T0293101

Empathic Leadership

Empathic leadership has become popular across industries including the challenging domain of elite sport. This book draws on the author's relevant research and experience and incorporates the words of leaders of teams to help to explain how empathy can help leaders to be successful in their work.

Seven aspects of empathy in leadership are described in detail, each illustrated with fascinating stories from male and female head coaches of teams competing at the highest levels of nine different team sports. The result is an authentic portrayal of what it takes to become an empathic leader. Exploring the philosophies and practices of empathic leadership, attention is paid to a range of important factors within leadership, including relationship management, building trust, and establishing a strong line of communication. This book also focuses on the importance of self-empathy as a starting point of empathic leadership, providing readers with ways to understand their own emotions and deep thoughts, and how they impact their leadership approach. Through this model, the author demonstrates how applying empathy in both work and life will enhance wellbeing, bring people together, and make leaders more influential and popular.

This book will be of interest to coaches in sport, training organisations including national governing bodies, recruiters, leaders across all industries, and anyone interested in the role of empathy in professional relationships.

Peter Sear is a psychologist, writer, and consultant. He gained his PhD from Loughborough University London, UK, with his thesis *Understanding Empathic Leadership in Elite Sport*. He also holds a master's degree in Jung and Post-Jungian Studies, a master's degree in Human Resource Management and Industrial Relations, and a BSc (Hons) in Psychology. He is a Member of the British Psychological Society and a Fellow of the Royal Society for Arts.

Empathic Leadership

Lessons from Elite Sport

PETER SEAR

LONDON AND NEW YORK

Designed cover image: Photo of Tor Thodesen, Rafael Toró, and Riku Selander by Niklas Günsberg

First published 2023
by Routledge
4 Park Square, Milton Park, Abingdon, Oxon OX14 4RN

and by Routledge
605 Third Avenue, New York, NY 10158

Routledge is an imprint of the Taylor & Francis Group, an informa business

British Library Cataloguing-in-Publication Data
A catalogue record for this book is available from the British Library

Library of Congress Cataloging-in-Publication Data
Names: Sear, Peter, author.
Title: Empathic leadership : lessons from elite sport / Peter Sear.
Description: Abingdon, Oxon ; New York, NY : Routledge, 2023. |
    Identifiers: LCCN 2022049081 (print) | LCCN 2022049082 (ebook) |
    ISBN 9781032349695 (hardback) | ISBN 9781032349459 (paperback) |
    ISBN 9781003324676 (ebook)
Subjects: LCSH: Leadership—Psychological aspects. | Empathy.
Classification: LCC BF637.L4 .S43 2023 (print) | LCC BF637.L4 (ebook) |
    DDC 158/.4—dc23/eng/20230201
LC record available at https://lccn.loc.gov/2022049081
LC ebook record available at https://lccn.loc.gov/2022049082

ISBN: 978-1-032-34969-5 (hbk)
ISBN: 978-1-032-34945-9 (pbk)
ISBN: 978-1-003-32467-6 (ebk)

DOI: 10.4324/9781003324676

Typeset in Dante and Avenir
by Apex CoVantage, LLC

This book has been printed on a non-white background, as advised by The British Dyslexia Association, to improve readability and limit the visual distortion effects experienced by some readers. Routledge is committed to provide equitable opportunities to every reader, and continuously strives to improve accessibility across our titles. If you have any feedback regarding this issue, we would like to hear from you.

Contents

Acknowledgements

I would like to thank Professor James Skinner for giving me the opportunity to base my PhD research into empathic leadership at Loughborough University London, and everyone else there who supported my work. This includes a wonderful community of fellow PhD researchers. Their enthusiasm for my work maintained my own.

I want to thank Jennifer for encouraging me with every idea I have, and for then putting up with me while I carry it out, which often takes longer than I suggested it would. I could not dream of sharing my life with more wonderful people than Jennifer and our daughters, Heidi and Isabel, who both impress and inspire me every day. I dedicate this book to the three of you.

I'm fortunate to have a supportive wider family, too. Thank you to my fantastic parents, Heather and Jim, for always being there, my brother, Andrew, who has set an impressive example of dedication in his pursuit of drumming excellence (although those years of sharing a room with him and his first drum kit I could have done without), and my sister, Sarah-Jayne, for buying us a dog during the writing of this book (which might explain a lot) and for being a cool auntie to our daughters.

Preface

If you lead, manage, or coach, or if you just want to gain a better understanding of people and improve your personal and/or professional relationships, this book will prove useful. I have utilised my research in elite sport, but the lessons in leadership will apply across many other industries. Sport leadership is merely a context in which to observe the power of empathy. However, the white waters of the elite sport environment certainly put the power of empathy in relationships to the test. Problems come from all kinds of directions, causing all kinds of stress on individuals and the bonds between them. If empathy proves beneficial in elite sport, it is likely to work wherever you are.

This book centres on my four years of researching the role of empathy in leadership at Loughborough University London. During this period, I spent time talking with 20 head coaches of teams working in nine different sports. At the time of writing, these head coaches are all still competing at the highest levels, whether it be international or top national level of their sport. I remain grateful to these people for giving me their time and sharing their knowledge. I assured them anonymity and so for the purposes of this book their names have not been used.

These head coaches consisted of eight nationalities, working in 11 different nations, in North America, Europe, and Australasia, and some have experience of working in Asia, Africa, and South America.

Wherever possible, I have used the words and stories told to me by these leaders to illustrate seven aspects of empathic leadership in elite sport.

Introduction

I met the head coach of a successful European football team recently, who told me how important empathy is in his work. I asked him how. He thought for a moment and then he said, "My academy coaches came to me and said, 'We have this great young player, and we think he should start training with the first team.' I've seen him play, and he does look good. 'Just look at his numbers,' they said. They told me how many goals he'd scored, his assists, how fast he can run, how high he can jump, everything like this. My first question was 'What sort of guy is he?' I want to know how he'd fit in with my squad. Would he build relationships? What are his motivations? How does he react under pressure? I want them to understand the whole person, and I think they try to do that, but they don't give me this information. Just numbers. They don't realise how much it matters. Before I let this kid train with us, I will spend time with him, talking to him about everything but football. I need to understand who he is and be able to predict how he will be when he's with us. This will be a work in progress. To understand people, you need to spend time with them. That's what my work is about. I understand my players' intentions and reactions. I know them inside out, so I know what they'll do when I ask something of them. I can see it before they do it." These are the words of an empathic leader.

After decades of a more dictatorial approach, current leaders of teams in elite sport are working more empathically, in closer relationships with their athletes.[1] During the last few years, I have learned from some of the most successful head coaches around. The consensus is that to have success as a leader in elite sport in the modern era, you must have an empathic approach. The head coaches who are leading with empathy are getting more out of

DOI: 10.4324/9781003324676-1

athletes. The environments they create are less likely to suffer from the kind of toxicity that has encompassed too many sporting organisations in the past. The lessons in this book will be supported by the words of the head coaches that I've met and the examples they have given.

Empathic leadership is based on the idea that it is impossible to connect with or motivate people if you cannot see the world from their perspective.[2] This idea has been tested in a variety of industries. A study of 6,731 managers from 38 countries found that empathic leadership enhanced performance.[3] Empathic leaders have been found to be more influential,[4] and they make working environments more humane, more considerate and less stressful, which is beneficial for wellbeing as well as performance.[5] Since it's clear that empathy offers leaders an advantage, it's unsurprising that there has been a surge in its popularity. In business,[6] the military,[7] politics,[8] medicine[9] and the competitive world of elite sport,[1, 10] the abilities to employ and express empathy have become an essential part of leadership.

This book focuses on seven aspects of empathic leadership, based on what I have learned from my research and work in elite sport. These components

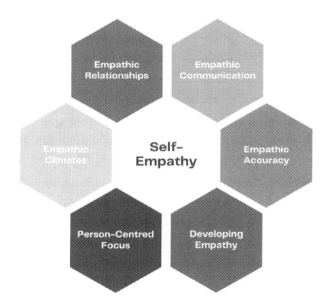

Figure 1. The seven aspects of empathic leadership

provide a template for leaders of teams in sport. However, this template can also be applied to leading people in other industries. The principles are the same. Whether you manage the proverbial paper merchant or lead an international corporation, your success will depend on your knowledge and understanding of people, their emotions, perspectives and intentions, as well as the relationships you have with them. It is in these vital areas that empathy will give you an advantage.

How Empathy Works for Leaders

Empathy stems from translations of the German word *Einfühlung* (in-feeling or feeling into) into the Greek *empatheia* (from pathos, meaning feeling). By feeling into the world of another, empathy brings deep understanding through a process of *decentering.*[11] Leaving their own perspective for a moment, the empathiser *imagines* and/or *feels* the world from another person's perspective. This allows the empathiser to gather valuable and intimate knowledge.

Since empathy conveys knowledge, it helps us to more fully understand others.[12] The more empathic individuals among us find it easy to become psychologically in tune with others' feelings and perspectives.[13] The empathic way of understanding is perhaps best summarised as an ability to read people.[14] This is an invaluable skill for anyone, particularly leaders.

Empathic understanding is the most human and natural form of data collection. For leaders, it offers an up-to-date and in-depth knowledge of other individuals in each context of their work. Mistakes are limited because the leader has the knowledge and understanding to respond appropriately. Empathic understanding is maintained through regular communication and close relationships. The empathic leader creates close bonds with those they lead which enable them to understand, serve understood needs, recognise talent and potential, and remain aware of a range of perspectives during decision making.[15]

An empathic leader doesn't only focus on the needs of team members, but the needs of all stakeholders, including their own.[6] Self-empathy is the starting point of empathic leadership. Understanding your own emotions and deep thoughts and how they impact your behaviour is necessary before endeavouring to understand the same in others.

Empathic leaders become skilled in understanding other people and are able to clearly communicate what they have understood. Sometimes this understanding of an athlete means the response a leader chooses appears to lack compassion. Empathy does not insist on or include a compassionate response.[16] An international lacrosse head coach explained: "Sometimes what a player needs is a kick up the backside, for want of a better expression, but you understand the person well enough to know that that is the best approach at that time. It's important not to confuse the idea of *empathy* being an arm round the shoulder all the time."

The Trend Towards Empathic Leadership

The trend towards empathic leadership in elite sport is highlighted by the comparisons made with how things were back when current head coaches were athletes. Empathic leaders working in elite sport today rarely have an empathic template to follow. Paradoxically, a complete lack of empathy from a head coach as an athlete can motivate someone to be an empathic leader, as a handball head coach explained to me: "I had very bad experiences, and I try to take a very different approach because of that. I was quite a difficult child, quite temperamental, and I worked with a coach with a one-rule-fits-all attitude. He was hard on me, and it was a very negative experience. When I went into coaching, I thought, right, I'm going to be the complete opposite to the coach I had. So, the way I deal with things as a coach has made me more empathic in life, and I learned from a bad example – a bully really."

An international hockey head coach was similarly unimpressed with the level of empathy and understanding of the head coaches he experienced as an athlete: "Their man management was appalling. Their knowledge of the game was good, but how they treated players was probably not how I thought it should have been done. I don't know if that impacted me wanting to be a coach, but I thought if I did become one, that's not the way to do it."

The head coaches that I've met have all said that sport leadership today requires a different kind of personality. Emotional and relationship skills such as empathy have become necessary and so a different kind of person is attracted to the role. An international hockey head coach told me, "I think some coaches from back then would struggle these days and wouldn't want to change. For me it's always been about the people, and it's always evolved to be the way you understand and engage." A football head coach working in North America went further, stressing that it's about "showing you care. Players need that in this day and age; you didn't see it ten or twenty years ago, but now it's part of management, it's what you need to do to get the best out of a player because it's what they need."

An international rugby union head coach explained to me that leadership of just a decade ago would now be considered unacceptable: "What a coach could say and how a coach could say it, ten years ago, you wouldn't last two minutes these days." An international football head coach described how the empathic leadership trend has evolved through his coaching career: "I'm 55, I've coached entry-level professionals, senior professionals, right up to and including the national team. Over the years, different styles evolved, and I've found I've been drawn to an appreciation of exactly what the player is thinking and going through. I grew up in the black-and-white days, we might like to call it, and as a budding professional, my existence was based in *fear* of the gaffer. If I didn't make him happy, I'm shit out of luck, you know what I mean? So, in those terms, I've had an evolution of becoming closer, not necessarily as an acquaintance, but a closer understanding of that individual or player. I need to know what they are feeling, both positively and to a large extent the stresses and potential negativity, and the failure and response mechanisms."

Whenever I talk about leadership with head coaches working today, they refer to these previous eras when the athlete would fear the head coach, whom they describe as typically autocratic or dictatorial. Head coaches have told me that their predecessors failed to appreciate that empathy makes leaders more influential and knowledgeable. The head coach of a football team explained that, by working in a more empathic way, "players no longer fear you; they respect you".

There were consequences to the leadership styles of the past. Only certain athlete personalities tolerated the kind of dictatorial leadership described, which means that talent was lost. Bright prospects were told they didn't fit, or chose to leave – lost to the club, nation, and sport.

A football head coach in North America told me, "Years ago, it was if Tommy doesn't toe the line, then Tommy is out, and needs to find another club. Whereas now it's not that way so much, the player has a lot more power." Similarly, the head coach of an English county cricket team said, "I think the environments I experienced as a player were far more *tell*. You learned on your feet, and they were far harsher. You could identify the people that that would work for. Whereas now, I think, the more scientific coaching has got, the more research people have done into human behaviour, it's understood that there's a real strength in working with them as human beings; making sure that they understand you care for them as people. You tend to get more in return."

I'd been curious as to whether the whole reason that leaders in sport had become more empathic was just to get more back from athletes, and because they'd seen the style bring success. Once a few head coaches had simultaneously been holding trophies in the air while being described as empathic, the new way of leading was sure to catch on. However, there is more to it than that. There has been a sea change across society, and societal expectations can be powerful influences in all industries. In sport, they change the way an athlete approaches their chosen profession and alter the expectations they have of coaches.

A recent survey, conducted across 29 countries, found that millennials desire a more open and collaborative relationship with their leaders.[17, 18] The generational shift in expectations is clear. Head coaches working today have noticed this within their squads, with younger members having very different expectations of them. The head coach of a women's football team told me, "The culture has changed. The millennials coming through need this empathic leadership style more. They expect it from me."

A football head coach working in New Zealand summarised these influences on leadership style, telling me, "I think it does come from players, and society, and *myself*." Which brings us back to the suggestion that a different kind of personality is suited to leadership roles in elite sport today. It has to be who they are as people, not just as leaders.

Empathic leadership is not a style that can be adopted unless empathy runs through the leader. An international rugby union head coach told me, "I class myself as a very empathic person. I'm always considering how my behaviour impacts the players." And an international lacrosse head coach said, "I'd like to think it's embedded in my coaching practice. But it's not about one or two examples – it's more pervasive than that, it's more of a mindset, a philosophy. It's embedded in everything you do. Being authentic is key. You can't just use empathy when you think an empathic approach is relevant – that is kind of missing the point. It's just you either are or you aren't."

Wherever in the world the head coaches I spoke with were working, and in whichever sport, they told me the same thing. A football coach in North America said, "I enjoy communicating, understanding people, caring for people. So it's a part of my coaching that I guess comes naturally because that's who I am as a person."

Some head coaches expressed their gratitude about the changes in society and sport leadership, and still wonder if they would have ever had a coaching career if they had not taken place. An ice hockey head coach in Europe told me, "I'm lucky to be a coach at this time. I'm not the sort of person who could have coached people the way they were expected to be coached 30 years ago. But I can be the right guy nowadays. I'm not sure how much the needs changed me, or how much I am the right fit for this need. But I'm glad to be in this business now."

Although empathic leadership is proving its worth across a growing number of industries, sport provides a unique context. Sport organisations are complex and chaotic – often said to be emotional cauldrons.[19] A key aspect to leadership in sport is managing the people and teams living and working inside these cauldrons. Emotions fluctuate within elite sport settings because of results, performances, the reactions of fans and interpretations of the media. This makes elite sport organisations incredibly unpredictable environments.

Unpredictable environments are known to exacerbate stress on individuals,[20] and organisational stressors have been described as a particular problem for sport performers.[21] Sports psychologists are often called in to work on the stress resulting from the interaction between individual athletes and the organisations they work for.[22] For athletes in elite sport, there are pressures attached to role-model status and lifestyle choices that are always with them, not just while they are at work. This constant stress and unpredictability heightens any paranoia they may have about selection and contracts, and creates the sense of a loss of control.[23] Athletes have the additional and ever-present pressures to perform, stay mentally and physically fit, injury-free and at a certain weight.[24] More than ever, athletes need the kind of understanding and care provided by a head coach who is an empathic leader.

There are further contextual complexities concerning elite sport and empathy. Although studies have shown that empathic leadership is positively related to organisational commitment,[25] it could be more complicated in sport. Athlete commitment may be directed towards an organisation, but it could be directed towards a specific head coach, certain team mates or even the sport as a whole.[19] This highlights the importance of empathy spreading throughout an organisation, and not just being about the head coach. The athlete needs to feel known and understood by leaders and owners of clubs if they are to remain committed to the organisation. This situation has been exaggerated in recent years, due to employment patterns and more regular movement of talent, making it more likely that an athlete will ultimately feel more committed towards the profession rather than the team or organisation they represent at any one time.[26]

In the present era, athletes are also drawn to commercial commitments through sponsorship, marketing and media opportunities,[27] which means their greatest commitment may be to their own brand. These changes present new challenges for sport leaders, who need to understand how the world looks through the eyes of athletes if they have any chance of maintaining their wellbeing and getting the best performances out of them.

With sport governance, the media, commercial activity and larger teams of athletes and assistants, head coaches have a greater number of relationships to manage in this complex and ever-changing environment than ever before. Only leaders with empathic relationship skills will remain in demand.

The Good News

As empathy has become more valued in professional arenas, aspiring leaders may be concerned that it is not one of their strengths. The good news is that nearly all of us are born with a capacity for empathy, which means that it can be developed.[8, 28] Empathic development usually begins in the second or third years of life and we can continue improving on our empathic ability all through our lives.[29]

Being *in tune* with another can be a positive or a negative experience. *Positive empathy* is where people share in one another's positive emotions, such as seeing a lottery winner celebrating on the television,[30] *Negative empathy* describes sharing in another's negative emotional state.[30, 31] This can lead to an experience of empathic distress, with motivation to reduce this distress by aiding an observed victim.[11]

In the empathic process, this feeling of *compassion* for another is often termed as *empathic concern*. The distress experienced isn't considered to be something too detrimental for the empathiser. It is obviously something familiar to anyone working in medicine. A study of medics revealed that empathy makes people more resilient and less likely to suffer burnout.[32] However, the impact of experiencing empathic distress will be different for each individual.

Ultimately, empathy provides us with knowledge, and reflecting on that determines our response, although there are times when we react before reflecting. Emotions can lead us to react in haste. Feeling the pain of someone else (affective empathy) may inspire violent acts that we will later regret.

Affective Empathy and Cognitive Empathy

Distinctions have been made concerning the exact experience of the empathiser. The empathic experience can be either an affective (sometimes referred to as emotional) or a cognitive understanding of other people's experiences.[33] Affective empathy provides a vicarious feeling response.[34, 35]

This means the empathiser feels the emotions of the other, similarly to how they feel them themselves. Cognitive empathy describes an awareness and understanding of the emotions of another, without feeling the same emotions.[36]

Affective empathy is automatic and occurs before conscious awareness, as a form of imitation, employing what have become known as mirror neurons.[37] This mimicking means that the emotions of another have been caught and the inner experience is being mirrored. Where these mirrored emotions are negative, the empathiser usually experiences feelings of empathic concern. Empathic concern for another usually leads us to act prosocially, as the *empathy–altruism hypothesis*[38] suggests. If we feel the negative emotions of another, we are motivated to act with care towards them. This is revealed in the care we show to our children or others we have close bonds with, such as friends and team members. It helps us to act more morally, whether it's within families, teams or large organisations. The urge is to respond helpfully to serve the other's needs.[39]

Empathy's altruistic motivations are comparable to a combined feeling of sympathy and compassion.[40] Sympathy represents the concern about another person's emotional state, without it having impacted one's own emotional state.[29] To be clear, to sympathise is to feel *for* but not *like* another individual. In other words, sympathy is incongruent, whereas empathy is congruent.[41] There are no mirror neurones involved in sympathy; if they become activated, sympathy has turned into empathy.

Compassion is the feeling that arises in witnessing another's suffering and that motivates a subsequent desire to help. Whereas empathy is about understanding and feeling the same emotions, compassion focuses on the concern for the plight of another. In this sense, empathy may precede compassion. It has been said that compassion consists of sympathy and pity.[42] Pity is about feeling for others who are in need due to conditions that are out of their control.[43] Both compassion and pity are more closely related to sympathy than empathy, as they are concerned with feelings towards someone's plight, rather than shared feelings or understanding of their perspective.[16] It is empathy that brings knowledge and understanding.

Empathy produces comforting and helping behaviours. Such helping behaviour is not seen as part of empathy, but rather a product of it. Therefore, empathy is a potential motivation for behaviour. The information gained, or data collected, may lead to a behaviour that is anything but altruistic. Empathy may be employed to enjoy the pain of others. It can provide the understanding required to undermine a competitor.[44] Therefore, for a leader in sport, empathy may provide a winning strategy against a rival.

It is unlikely that a leader in sport will have a close relationship with the opposition's leader. They may know them well, but not communicate regularly enough to be sharing emotions vicariously. If this is the case, understanding the emotions, thoughts and perspectives of an opposition head coach can be achieved more easily through cognitive empathy.

An example of this kind of cognitive empathy is *perspective taking* or *mentalising*.[45] Perspective taking does not focus on feeling emotions, but it can achieve an understanding of the emotions of the other.[16] Cognitive empathy is often said to be cold and emotionless, and some refuse to accept that it is really empathy at all.[46] It may not involve feeling, but it does involve imagining and provides an accurate picture of the inner world of another.

Perspective taking can be useful for those wishing to gain victory over others, or to do harm to them. Some acts of cruelty are facilitated by high levels of empathy.[47] This includes the typical manipulation of others seen in psychopathy.[48] It is suggested that psychopaths employ cognitive empathy in order to understand the feelings of others, without actually feeling or suffering from those feelings themselves.[16, 48]

Cognitive empathy can also be employed to help with negotiations. Any negotiator who fails to understand the other party's interests will struggle to obtain the best outcome for themselves.[46] Precisely understanding another's thoughts and feelings, a skill appropriately known as empathic accuracy, is sure to help in predicting their next move.[49] Cognitive empathy has been shown to be employed more than affective empathy in empathic accuracy tasks.[50] If an accurate understanding of an opponent's strategy is critical for success, then perspective taking is a useful skill to perfect.[45] Those who have concerns about the emotional overload of empathising will prefer to *think with* rather than *feel with* other people, particularly their rivals.

Leadership in the political world offers us examples of the dangers of lacking empathic understanding of adversaries. Whether feeling with or thinking with another, some knowledge of them is essential to achieve empathic accuracy and an understanding of intentions. This reinforces the need for close relationships. Before the Second World War, as well as Prime Minister Neville Chamberlain, Britain sent Lord Halifax and Sir Nevile Henderson to meet Adolf Hitler in attempts to gauge his intentions. Having had no prior relationship with Hitler, gaining an empathic understanding through perspective taking alone proved impossible. All three men returned certain that Hitler did not intend to go to war.[51]

The ability to accurately understand the mental states of others is something that psychologists often refer to as theory of mind (ToM).[52] However, ToM ability appears to vary from person to person. Like most things, practice brings improvement, and reading fiction is often suggested to be good practice. Research supports this. Subjects who score higher for ToM tend to be more avid readers of fiction than those who record lower scores.[53] Films, novels, plays and television dramas also offer the opportunity to practise perspective taking by projecting ourselves into the social interactions and emotional experiences of others.[53]

Whether you are trying to understand the perspective of a real person or a literary character, there is something else to keep in mind when practising empathy. Empathy is not about putting oneself in another's shoes; rather, it is about imagining what it is like to be the other person.[54] Cognitive empathy insists on obtaining the perspective of another person rather than remaining egocentric.

Not only does cognitive empathy require us to stop being ourselves for a moment and see the world from another's situation, but it also requires us to pay close attention to that person. This demands skills such as listening. By actively listening to people, we are more able to remove our egocentric bias and get closer to the genuine perspective of another.[55]

It has been claimed that, in sport, empathy offers the most direct route to building relationships.[56] Successful head coaches of the modern era understand and empower their team members through these relationships.[57] The tenure of head coaches in elite sport is often short-lived. Ultimately, it relies on understanding and responding to the needs of others.[58] Empathy is contagious; with mutual understanding, leaders can ensure team members are in tune with their ideas and goals.[59]

Without empathy, head coaches cannot develop and nurture strong relationships. This negatively impacts the ability to motivate and encourage team members. Without empathy, leaders will be unable to understand the intentions of their rivals to accurately predict the performances of their own and rival athletes. And without empathy, a leader will be unable to understand and manage the emotions in the working environment. With so many relationships to maintain, a head coach must employ empathy in a multitude of directions. This is why empathy has become a crucial aspect of being a head coach in elite sport.[60]

Elite-level sport provides a high-performance context for the role of empathy in leadership at a time when an appreciation of emotional skills in the sport industry seems to be growing. If used intelligently, empathically gained knowledge will contribute to improved decision making and to the understanding of how others might think and respond when in a particular mood or situation.

Empathic leaders understand the contagious nature of emotions. The powerful combination of empathy and positive emotional contagion can offer inspiration and motivation to team members. Empathic leaders remain aware that emotions are adaptive responses to the demands of a challenging environment. They are dependent on the behaviours and emotions of others, which highlights the importance of developing empathy throughout teams and organisations. Head coaches who develop relationships based on empathy, will find themselves leading the best-performing teams.

Notes

1. Tóth, L. & Reinhardt, M. (2019). Factors underlying the coach–athlete relationship: The importance of empathy as a trait in coaching. In K. A. Moore, K. Kaniasty, P. Arenas-Landgrave & P. Buchwald (Eds). *Stress and Anxiety – Contributions of the STAR Award Winners* (pp. 151–167). LogosVerlag. https://books.google.co.uk/books?hl=en&lr=&id=SJ6hDwAAQBAJ&oi=fnd&pg=PA151&dq=related:woJ7FY4-EbYJ:scholar.google.com/&ots=MRmz3UARm-&sig=HYCkh0kGGk6wLnGFG5TmUI-4lJ0&redir_esc=y#v=onepage&q&f=false

2. Buckingham, D. L. (2014). *The empathic leader: An effective management model for enhancing morale and increasing workplace productivity – Workbook*. RHCS Publishing.

3. Gentry, W. A., Weber, T. J. & Sadri, G. (2007). Empathy in the workplace: A tool for effective leadership. *Center for Creative Leadership*, 1–13. doi:10.1007/s11664-015-4010-3

4. Shootman, A. (2018). How empathy makes leaders of modern work more influential. *Done Right*. www.workfront.com/blog/empathy-leaders

5. Costa, G. & Glinia, E. (2003). Empathy and sport tourism services: A literature review. *Journal of Sport and Tourism*, 8(4), 284–292.

6. Kock, N., Mayfield, M., Mayfield, J., Sexton, S. & De La Garza, L. M. (2019). Empathetic leadership: How leader emotional support and understanding influences follower performance. *Journal of Leadership and Organizational Studies*, 26(2), 217–236.

7. McDougall, J. (2019). Empathic leadership: Understanding the human domain. *English Military Review*, November–December. www.armyupress.army.mil/Portals/7/military-review/Archives/English/ND-19/McDougall-Empathetic-Leadership.pdf

8. Lanzoni, S. (2018). *Empathy: A history*. Yale University Press.

9. Wetterauer, U. & Ruhl, S. (2011). Empathische Führung: Veränderung positiv gestalte [Empathic leadership: Shaping positive change]. *Der Urologe*, 50, 1578–1583.

10. Sear, P. (2021). *Understanding empathic leadership in sport*. PhD thesis, Loughborough University London. https://repository.lboro.ac.uk/articles/thesis/Understanding_empathic_leadership_in_sport/14958750

11. Redmond, M. V. (1989). The functions of empathy (decentering) in human relations. *Human Relations, 42*(7), 593–605.

12. Wondra, J. D. & Ellsworth, P. C. (2015). An appraisal theory of empathy and other vicarious emotional experiences. *Psychological Review, 122*(3), 411–428.

13. Decety, J. & Lamm, C. (2006). Human empathy through the lens of social neuroscience. *Scientific World Journal, 6*, 1146–1163.

14. Korn Ferry Institute. (2014). The limits of empathy for executives. www.kornferry.com/institute/limits-empathy-executive

15. Tzouramani, E. (2017). Leadership and empathy. In J. Marques & S. Dhiman (Eds), *Leadership today: Practices for personal and professional development* (pp. 197–216). Springer. doi:10.1007/978-3-319-31036-7_11

16. Cuff, B. M. P., Brown, S. J., Taylor, L. & Howat, D. J. (2016). Empathy: A review of the concept. *Emotion Review, 8*(2), 144–153.

17. Marques, J. (2015). The changed leadership landscape: What matters today. *Journal of Management Development, 34*(10), 1310–1322.

18. Deloitte. (2016). The Deloitte Millennial Survey. www2.deloitte.com/al/en/pages/about-deloitte/articles/2016-millennialsurvey.html

19. Wagstaff, C. & Hanton, S. (2017). Emotions in sport organizations. In C. Wagstaff & S. Hanton (Eds), *The organizational psychology of sport* (pp. 33–61). Routledge.

20. Hou, X., Liu, Y., Sourina, O., Tan, Y. R. E., Wang, L. & Mueller-Wittig, Y. (2015). EEG based stress monitoring. In *2015 IEEE International Conference on Systems, Man, and Cybernetics* 3110–3115. IEEE. doi:10.1109/SMC.2015.540

21. Arnold, R., Wagstaff, C. R. D., Steadman, L. & Pratt, Y. (2017). The organisational stressors encountered by athletes with a disability. *Journal of Sports Sciences, 35*(12), 1187–1196.

22. Woodman, T. & Hardy, L. A (2001). Case study of organizational stress in elite sport. *Journal of Applied Sport Psychology, 13*(2), 207–238.

23. Coakley, J. (1992). Burnout among adolescent athletes: A personal failure or social problem? *Sociology of Sport Journal, 9*(3), 271–285.

24. Larkin, D., Levy, A. R., Marchant, D. & Martin, C. R. (2017). When winners need help: Mental health in elite sport. *The Psychologist*, August, 42–46.

25. Ashkanasy, N. M. & Humphrey, R. T. H. (2011). A multi-level view of leadership and emotions: leading with emotional labor. In A. Bryman, D. Collinson, K. Grint, B. Jackson & M. Uhl-Bien (Eds), *Sage handbook of leadership* (pp. 363–377). Sage Publications.

26. Lee, K., Carswell, J. J. & Allen, N. J. (2000). A meta-analytic review of occupational commitment: Relations with person- and work-related variables. *Journal of Applied Psychology*, *85*(5), 799–811.

27. Wagg, S. (2007). Angels of us all? Football management, globalization and the politics of celebrity. *Soccer and Society*, *8*(4), 440–458.

28. Engen, H. G. & Singer, T. (2013). Empathy circuits. *Current Opinion in Neurobiology*, *23*(2), 275–282.

29. Decety, J. (2010). The neurodevelopment of empathy in humans. *Developmental Neuroscience*, *32*(4), 257–267.

30. Morelli, S. A., Lieberman, M. D. & Zaki, J. (2015). The emerging study of positive empathy. *Social and Personality Psychology Compass*, *9*(2), 57–68.

31. Andreychik, M. R. & Migliaccio, N. (2015). Empathizing with others' pain versus empathizing with others' joy: Examining the Separability of positive and negative empathy and their relation to different types of social behaviors and social emotions. *Basic and Appled Social Psychology*, *37*(5), 274–291.

32. Yuguero, O., Ramon Marsal, J., Esquerda, M., Vivanco, L. & Soler-González, J. (2016). Association between low empathy and high burnout among primary care physicians and nurses in Lleida, Spain. *European Journal of General Practice*, *23*(1), 4–10. doi:10.1080/13814788.2016.1233173.

33. Hatfield, E., Rapson, R. L. & Le, L. (2013). Emotional contagion and empathy. In J. Decety & W. Ickes (Eds), *The Social Neuroscience of Empathy* (pp. 19–30). MIT Press. doi:10.7551/mitpress/9780262012973.003.0003

34. Hoffman, M. L.(2000). *Empathy and moral development*. Cambridge University Press. doi:10.1017/CBO9780511805851

35. Dziobek, I., Rogers, K., Fleck, S., Bahnemann, M., Heekeren, H. R., Wolf, O. T. & Convit, A. (2008). Dissociation of cognitive and emotional empathy in adults with Asperger syndrome using the Multifaceted Empathy Test (MET). *Journal of Autism and Developmental Disorders*, *38*(3), 464–473.

36. Blanke, E. S., Rauers, A. & Riediger, M. (2016). Does being empathic pay off? Associations between performance-based measures of empathy and social adjustment in younger and older women. *Emotion*, *16*(5), 671–683.

37. Burch, G., Bennett, A., Humphrey, R., Batchelor, J. & Cairo, A. (2016). Unraveling the complexities of empathy research: A multi-level model of empathy in organizations. In *Research on Emotion in Organizations* vol. 12 (pp. 169–189). Emerald Group Publishing.

38. Batson, C. D. (1991). *The altruism question: Toward a social psychological answer*. Lawrence Erlbaum, Associates.

39. Senbel, M. (2005). *Empathic leadership in sustainability planning*. PhD thesis, University of British Columbia. doi:10.14288/1.0092304

40. Singer, T. & Klimecki, O. M. (2014). Empathy and compassion. *Current Biology*, 24(18), R875–R878.
41. Hein, G. & Singer, T. (2008). I feel how you feel but not always: The empathic brain and its modulation. *Current Opinion in Neurobiology*, 18(2), 153–158.
42. Goetz, J. L., Keltner, D. & Simon-Thomas, E. (2010). Compassion: An evolutionary analysis and empirical review. *Psychological Bulletin*, 136(3), 351–374.
43. Weiner, B., Graham, S. & Chandler, C. (1982). Pity, anger, and guilt: An attributional analysis. *Personality and Social Psychology Bulletin*, 8(2), 226–232.
44. Hodges, S. & Biswas-Diener, R. (2007). Balancing the empathy expense account: Strategies for regulating empathic response. In T. Farrow & P. Woodruff (Eds), *Empathy in mental illness* (pp. 389–407). Cambridge University Press. doi:10.1017/CBO9780511543753.022
45. Gilin, D., Maddux, W. W., Carpenter, J. & Galinsky, A. D. (2013). When to use your head and when to use your heart: The differential value of perspective-taking versus empathy in competitive interactions. *Personality and Social Psychology Bulletin*, 39(1), 3–16.
46. Galinsky, A. D., Maddux, W. W., Gilin, D. & White, J. B. (2008). Why it pays to get inside the head of your opponent. *Psychological Science*, 19(4), 378–384.
47. Breithaupt, F. & Hamilton, A. B. B. (2019). *The dark sides of empathy*. Cornell University Press.
48. Babiak, P. & Hare, R. D. (2006). *Snakes in suit : When psychopaths go to work*. Regan Books.
49. Lorimer, R. (2013). The development of empathic accuracy in sports coaches. *Journal of Sport Psychology in Action*, 4(1), 26–33.
50. Mackes, N. K., Golm, D., O'Daly, O. G., Sarkar, S., Sonuga-Barke, E. J. S., Fairchild, G. & Mehta, M. A. (2018). Tracking emotions in the brain – Revisiting the Empathic Accuracy Task. *Neuroimage*, 178, 677–686.
51. Gladwell, M. (2019). *Talking to strangers: What we should know about the people we don't know*. Little, Brown.
52. Astington, J., Harris, P. & Olson, D. (1990). *Developing theories of mind*. Cambridge University Press.
53. Mar, R. A. & Oatley, K. (2008). The function of fiction is the abstraction and simulation of social experience. *Perspectives on Psychological Science*, 3(3), 173–192.
54. Main, A., Walle, E. A., Kho, C. & Halpern, J. (2017). The interpersonal functions of empathy: A relational perspective. *Emotion Review*, 9(4), 358–366.
55. Eyal, T., Steffel, M. & Epley, N. (2018). Perspective mistaking: Accurately understanding the mind of another requires getting perspective, not taking perspective. *Journal of Personality and Social Psychology*, 114(5), 547–571.

56. Rollnick, S., Fader, J. S., Breckon, J. & Moyers, T. B. (2019). *Coaching athletes to be their best: Motivational interviewing in sports.* Guilford Press.
57. Kerr, J. M. (2013). *Legacy.* Constable.
58. Côté, J. & Gilbert, W. (2009). An integrative definition of coaching effectiveness and expertise. *International Journal of Sports Science and Coaching,* 4(3), 307–323.
59. Galipeau, J. & Trudel, P. (2006). Athlete learning in a community of practice: Is there a role for the coach? In R. L. Jones (Ed.), The sports coach as educator: Re-conceptualising sports coaching (pp. 7–94). Routldge.
60. Hanold, M. T. (2011). Leadership, women in sport, and embracing empathy. *Advancing Women in Leadership, 31,* 160–165.

Self-Empathy

1

As an empathic leader, you will constantly engage in the worlds of others. You will experience emotions vicariously and this will bring a valuable understanding of others' experiences. However, care is required to not confuse another's emotional experience with your own. This problem can easily surface without you being consciously aware of it, and it can inhibit your wellbeing, as well as your performance as a leader. An empathic leader works on understanding their inner world and learns to manage their emotions and the emotions of those who surround them. By doing so, a leader will improve their decision making, quality of relationships, and chances of success.

Understanding Your Inner World

Improving levels of self-awareness allows a head coach to disentangle the emotional state of their own mind from the minds of others.[1] Self-empathy will help you to develop agency, as you become more aware of yourself as being the creator of your own behaviour, dreams, thoughts, and feelings.[2] Gaining knowledge of your own inner world will help you to avoid errors of judgement related to your deepest emotions, or emotions that belong to other people.

The head coach of a successful ice hockey team offered the following example. Referring to a pre-match discussion he had with his coaching staff, he said: "We had an important game. We had a practice on the ice before that game. We go to the coaches' room and agree we are just not happy with what

DOI: 10.4324/9781003324676-2

we've seen or felt out there. 'Oh, we look so nervous,' I said. When you feel that, you need to consider, are you sure it's really the players and it's not you? We realised it was us. We, the coaches were nervous, not the players."

This level of self-awareness and reflection is necessary to understand the true needs of a team. Empathic understanding insists on you distinguishing the independent source of the experienced emotions.[3] By reacting to the emotions that he was experiencing, without reflecting on them, the head coach could have given a counterproductive pre-match-talk by suggesting to his players they were nervous.

The probability of inner worlds merging or being confused is exacerbated because empathic leaders tend to enjoy closer relationships with those they lead. In close relationships, steeped in empathy, people can become immersed in each other's worlds. The immersion in another's world can have physical as well as emotional repercussions.

If you've been involved in sport at all, even as a spectator, you will have noticed yourself, other fans, or coaches on the touchline mirroring the body movement required of an athlete in a particular moment. This inclination to participate in somebody else's movement is known as *kinaesthetic empathy*.[4] For a coach, this might manifest as reaching out to catch a ball, or movements of the head, as if heading a football. The more invested you are, or the closer you feel to an athlete, the more likely you are to physically move. You understand the required action, your body becomes their body, and you act it out, without a conscious intention to do so. This is the power of empathy; it can influence your body as well as your mind.

Any empathic experience will enhance your knowledge. If you become another person for a moment, emotionally or physically, you gain a better understanding of their perspective. This knowledge provides opportunities for leaders to help to modify thought processes and behaviours that may be sabotaging goals or threatening wellbeing. Acknowledging these experiences is part of your journey towards understanding what is going on in your inner world and how it influences your thoughts, behaviours, and decisions. Untangling your emotions will help both you *and* those you lead.

Leadership decisions emanate from a combination of emotions and cognition. The most challenging aspect of self-empathy is accessing the emotions and intentions that live below your consciousness. Delving into the lower reaches of your mind may seem a daunting prospect. Who knows what might be lurking down there? Despite the innate curiosity of human beings, as a species we have a natural fear of the unknown.

Over two-thirds of the Earth's surface is covered by water, yet as a species human beings have chosen to explore outer space before understanding much of the life and activity at the depths of Earth's oceans. It's possible that we find deep water more intimidating than deep space. We choose to focus on something we can see, just by looking up at night, rather than something we have limited sensory contact with. We would have to venture to the bottom of the ocean to see what is there; even then, it would be dark, and our visibility limited. We can see almost nothing from the surface.

The psychologist Carl Jung used water as a symbol of the unconscious mind, a reservoir of feelings, thoughts, and experiences located outside of our awareness, which continue to influence behaviour. Jung was following in the footsteps of Freud, who believed in releasing the *unconscious* thoughts, memories, and feelings that have a negative impact on our being. Freud believed that dark, supressed thoughts, difficult to access, may surface as so-called Freudian slips of the tongue or symbolically in dreams. However, Jung's view of the unconscious was more positive, seeing it as a pool of potential development, full of possibilities.

These two pioneers of psychology inspired a variety of psychotherapeutic styles and techniques aimed at exploring the unconscious. Therapeutic and analytic avenues are worth considering if you are committed to gaining knowledge and understanding of your inner world, but a perfect understanding of the unconscious mind will never be possible. As soon as you know something, it no longer resides in your unconscious, and your unconscious is never empty.

Sitting between the unconscious and the conscious is the preconscious part of your mind. Contemporary psychologists view the preconscious mind as a part of consciousness that we are unaware of in a moment but which remains influential. Your preconscious contains sensory information, feelings, and recalled memories, all of which can be consciously accessed by focusing your attention. You could be having a deep conversation in the street when someone walks by in a football shirt. You may hardly have noticed the person who has passed you, but when asked to recall them, a picture appears in your mind. You might recall the colour of their shirt and then further details that confirm which team's shirt it was.

Such pieces of information – that you would have been otherwise unaware of – can influence the way you feel and, therefore, the way you lead. The shirt may have been of a team that you recently lost to, giving you a negative feeling, or the team you coach, adding to the feelings of expectation upon you. By being aware, you can reflect on how you feel and choose to see the incident for what it is – just a stranger in a shirt. Awareness can limit the impact on feeling. This is your cognition interacting with your emotions.

A fountain of knowledge and understanding can be found just by tapping into what is really going on in your inner world, and this fountain grows with practice. By being mindful of our experiences and surroundings, we can examine influences that we were previously unaware of, and which might be inhibiting decision making and chances of success.

Certain habits provide pathways to detect these influences if we are motivated enough to follow them. At some point in each day, you will naturally disengage from the rest of the world. Your mind may wander while you're boiling the kettle, or you might more deliberately plan a quiet moment to reflect on your thoughts. However they occur, these moments should be welcomed. This may not be as easy as you think. Research suggests that few of us welcome time spent allowing our thoughts to surface. In fact, many of us will do anything to prevent this from happening.

A series of psychological studies at the University of Virginia demonstrated that some people will go as far as choosing an electric shock over being left alone with their thoughts. Timothy Wilson and colleagues asked undergraduate volunteers to take part in a study of thinking periods.[5] Subjects were placed in sparsely furnished rooms and asked to pack away any belongings, including phones and pens. They were presented with one of two tests, which lasted between six and 15 minutes. Some were asked to think about whatever they wanted; others chose from prompts, such as *think about playing a sport*. The subjects were told to rate their experience. In both the free-thinking and planned-prompt scenarios, around half reported not finding the experience enjoyable.

The study was repeated in the comfort of the homes of the volunteers. Even in more familiar surroundings, the results were similar. Subjects reported that although they often enjoyed time alone, doing things such as reading and listening to music, just thinking was not enjoyable, or even tolerable. When Wilson decided to take the study a step further, his subjects were left alone in a room with a button. They could push the button to shock themselves and put an end to their session. Two-thirds of men and a quarter of women chose to shock themselves to get out of having to sit quietly and allow their thoughts to surface.

Wilson's work reveals the magnitude of the challenge, particularly in this technological age. With social media at your fingertips, you need never be alone with your thoughts. As human beings, we are built to interact with our external world. It is far easier for us to be doing something in that regard than to do nothing but observe our thoughts, even if the former has a negative impact on us and the latter has a positive one. An awareness of the advantages of allowing yourself to daydream will perhaps be enough motivation for you to overcome the kinds of inhibitions experienced by Wilson's subjects.

If it is not something you have done until now, don't worry. It is certainly possible to learn to be alone with your thoughts. It may not be a matter of planning moments but of simply allowing it to happen. Daydreaming occurs spontaneously. This is how your mind works: it focuses and then may become distracted until you choose to bring it back to focus. The solutions you need may be found where these states collide. Daydreaming brings you closer to your inner world and releases the creativity that dwells there. Ideas, solutions, and winning strategies lie in wait. It can also present you with an image of something to strive for.

'I have a daydream' may not have the same ring to it, but when Martin Luther King Jr talked of having a *dream*, he was describing a vision, rather than a dream he had during sleep. His vision provided an image, for himself and others, of what the world could be like. If we want to pursue something, we need to have an image of it. Daydreams bring us those images. A leader's daydreamed image may become a focal point for a whole squad of athletes, a club, or organisation. This is also something a leader can encourage in those they lead.

> All men dream: but not equally. Those who dream by night in the dusty recesses of their minds wake up in the day to find it was vanity, but the dreamers of the day are dangerous men, for they may act their dreams with open eyes, to make it possible.
>
> T.E. Lawrence, *Seven Pillars of Wisdom: A Triumph* (1922)

Dr Jay Granat, a psychotherapist, hypnotherapist, and coach, recommends daydreaming to his clients. To those who find it difficult, he suggests background music to help. Granat believes athletes should believe in the power of using daydreams to visualise positive results. He calls this Cognitive Behavioural Dream Therapy.[6] Athletes are encouraged to daydream about how they wish to perform. This may involve envisioning a finish line or of just running fast. The theory is that daydreaming can help you to get in touch with your deeper desires and instil greater belief. You've seen it, so you know it's possible – probable even. It's going to happen. You can see where you're headed.

Granat's theory resonates with what head coaches have expressed to me. An international rugby union coach told me, "Even during games, I like to get away from the other coaches. Sometimes, there'll be a break in play, or as we are waiting for the half to start, and I'll stare at nothing. And that's when things come up, ideas and plays I see in my mind, that have never happened. They are things I've dreamed up and could be something that makes the difference on the day. That wouldn't happen if I was sat talking to my assistants."

When accepted, daydreaming becomes habitual. Before you have realised what you are doing, you have gained a little more understanding of how you really feel, of how your feelings are influencing your decisions, or you've come up with a game-winning strategy. Obviously, care needs to be taken with this. No doubt, there are times when daydreaming would be inappropriate. A head coach of a women's football team explains: "It's no good me standing in front of my squad and them waiting for me to talk, and I'm staring into space. It's the same with them. I have a young squad and you can see their attention span isn't great. They lack focus. If you speak to the group as a whole, you can see them zone out. And so I tend to work with smaller groups."

However, when the time is right, daydreaming can be a great source of creativity and can help to solve the problems that stand in the way of success. This is true across industries. Daydreaming is now being actively encouraged within some of the most successful organisations in the world.[7, 8]

When I met the head coach of a cricket team, he associated daydreaming with being in a *flow state* (an optimal psychological state[9]), which banishes inhibitive thoughts, stopping our conscious mind from blocking our desired path. "It's all the clutter that's in your head," he told me. "That you can park. The goalposts can change because of what's between the ears, and that's what fascinates me."

Another way of gaining access to your preconscious, and possibly unconscious, thoughts, popular with head coaches in elite sport, is to meditate. Meditation is also great for your wellbeing. It's become widely accepted that meditation reduces stress, heart rate, blood pressure, and anxiety, and it has also been shown to enhance relationships between athletes and coaches.[10] Therefore, meditation is good for you and your leadership. It is becoming increasingly popular with head coaches in elite sport: "I probably meditate two or three times a week," a rugby union head coach told me. "It's become a regular exercise for my mind, similar to the way we exercise our body in sport."

Suspending judgement is an important aspect of self-empathy. As you meditate, you can put your own opinions and values on the bench, moving between your inner and outer worlds without prejudice. Judgements can threaten your wellbeing and can emanate from either world. As a leader in elite sport, you may live in the public eye, where everyone has an opinion on what you're doing, including hardworking journalists. When you are criticised in newspapers or have your coaching style or strategy openly questioned on TV or on social media, it may lead to tension. It's important to understand that it is your interpretation of another person's words that is creating this tension, and that maybe you should alter the thought process that leads to this. After all, it was bound to happen. Was it ever likely everyone would agree with how you lead? Are your critics aware of the full picture? And so is there any value in their judgements? Is there really anything to be gained from them?

Consider your emotional reaction to your inner and outer worlds, and the consequences of these reactions. Take your time. Suspend your judgement. Open your mind to possibilities and perspectives that are beyond your emotional reactions. Meditation can help with all of this.

There are various methods of beginning meditation. The head coach of an international volleyball team recommended an approach that focuses on observing your mind and feeling into your body. He believes that every mental state has a bodily expression that can be observed. His practice of meditation proceeds as follows: "Shut your eyes. Take some deep breaths and relax. Starting at the tips of your toes, conduct a body scan. Don't rush this. Notice that each of your body parts have stories to tell. Your feet, your knees . . . Stories of fatigue, tension, nerves, or relaxation. This awareness and acknowledgement of your body's stories will increase your understanding of your state of mind. There's a certain kind of strength that comes from that."

The strength that this head coach is referring to is the kind of strength that comes from integrating thoughts and emotions, which dampens down reflexive reactions. As a leader, you need to be aware of your emotions; it is the first step of learning to manage them.

Managing Your Emotions

You cannot recognise the emotions of those you lead without acknowledging and managing your own. Emotions are not always on your side. They can be your best friends and yet the worst of enemies. They can be motivational and need not be controlling. Take anger, something we all feel from time to time. Acting out our feelings of anger without applying logic is unlikely to serve us or our cause well. We might go around hitting people and end up in trouble. Even once you've recognised its destructive tendencies, your anger can be acted out to protect your ego; it may be seen as a demonstration of strength. As a leader, you are constantly observed by others and reacting to insults without a display of anger may be perceived as weak. No leader wants to feel undermined. But there is always a bigger picture.

Empathic leaders know how to transcend their own emotions in pursuit of the ambitions they have for their team or organisation. Far from making you look strong, failing to manage your own emotions will leave you imprisoned by them. In prison, you have little power, but you still have choices to make about what you do with your emotions.

It says much about the late Nelson Mandela, a man imprisoned for nearly a third of his life, that he is remembered as an embodiment of both freedom and leadership. It is often said that a great leader focuses on what he/she can control. To a significant extent, this is what is going on internally. When Mandela lost his freedom, he had 27 years of breaking rocks, poor clothing, and no family contact. He slept in a room he could barely lie down in. Mandela could have spent the whole of his prison time being angry; instead, he used his time for what he (citing Marcus Aurelius) referred to as *Conversations with Myself*.[11]

Mandela knew anger and its destructiveness well. He learned to control his impulses through his experiences as a younger man. Reflecting on what and how he felt, and how his emotions might get in the way of his dreams of what South Africa might become, Mandela set upon a more stoic approach. He believed that his whole continent needed discipline and self-control and wanted to become an example to follow. He knew that there would be no chance of progress for South Africa if two factions were held apart by hate and yearnings for revenge. His emotions told him that what was going on was wrong, but he realised that the answer was cooperation rather than violence.

Mandela began to do things in prison that puzzled his fellow inmates. He learned Afrikaans and studied the culture and beliefs of his oppressors. He became more empathic, increasing his understanding of his opposition's perspective, and he practised cooperation, forming friendships with his guards. These relationships became close, which facilitated Mandela's empathy, allowing his understanding of his adversaries to grow deeper still.

After his interview with Mandela in July 2008, Richard Stengel formulated a series of eight Mandela lessons.[12] The sixth lesson – 'Appearances matter – and remember to smile' – acknowledges Mandela's stoic approach and where he gained understanding of felt emotions, without allowing them to dominate his behaviour.

Mandela's ever-present smile became an emblem of hope and strength. He understood that this appearance would pave the way for stronger influence, respect, and support. He was demonstrating empathic leadership and the strength that comes with it. It proved to be a winning strategy. His calm and warm appearance may have been described by some to be *soft leadership*, yet it proved strong enough to defeat half a century of Apartheid.

Mandela's success serves as a reminder to all leaders of the importance of managing your emotions. Not only did he manage to fulfil his dreams, but his calmness also helped him to maintain his wellbeing.

Maintaining Your Wellbeing

Understanding your deeper thoughts and emotions is crucial to maintaining wellbeing, and your wellbeing is critical to your leadership. As a leader, you are likely to feel a great deal of responsibility for the wellbeing of those you lead, but this shouldn't be at the expense of your own. Studies have shown that people will prioritise their pet's wellbeing over their own, and possibly the most caring of professionals – nurses – are renowned for self-neglect and burnout.[13]

Monitoring your wellbeing requires self-awareness. Self-empathy focuses on understanding, monitoring, and meeting your own needs, rather than suffering from the consequences of ignoring them. Maintaining psychological wellbeing is a challenge for everyone, but some worry that empathic leadership may exacerbate that challenge. The more time spent in the world of others, the less time a leader can be present in their own world. Preventing the self from being the self can be a pathway to burnout.[14]

In close relationships, empathy should be used economically and rationally.[15] Concern about this threat can motivate a leader to reduce their empathy,[16] but this will inhibit the benefits of empathy, understanding others' situations.[17] By regulating your empathy, or employing cognitive rather than affective empathy, a healthy balance becomes achievable.

It has also been reported that a vicarious experience of emotions can be a good thing. Sharing the emotions of someone who is celebrating success can have a positive effect on a leader's wellbeing. Of course, there are cases where empathy can induce overwhelming feelings of distress. Sharing negative emotions can come with a cost and, if dominant and sustained, may lead to burnout.[14] A European football head coach described to me the consequences of a leader's emotions getting out of control: "I was an assistant coach to a head coach who was becoming burnt out and wasn't doing anything about it. He came in one day and was running, screaming, and shouting things that didn't make sense; the emotional pressure had got to him. The players were like, 'What's going on?' And they lost all respect for him, and it became a bit of a joke, and that meant results went downhill from that point. The belief had gone, the respect had gone, everything had gone. That was just based on how he behaved that day."

Despite the concerns about empathy being draining for leaders, the head coaches who I've discussed this with refuse to see empathic leadership as a burden. These coaches claim that burnout will arise due to workload and a lack of breaks, not because of empathy. For head coaches in elite sport, the hours do seem excessive. An international head coach told me, "I suffered burnout. I was working 70 hours a week and there was no balance in my life, but I'm not sure it was to do with how much empathy I have." This head coach also described other pressures: "If you take the recent competition, I was completely broken, because for some competitions we have two months in a hotel with one another. It's too much. I send them back to their clubs. It's constant. An illness goes through everyone. If someone's having a bad day, it impacts others. There's also a brilliant side, but you do get emotionally drained. Although I've always been able to compartmentalise the media, for example. That impacts my family more than me. It's very rare that someone comes to you with loads of positives. It's always problems. Problem with the physio, the eggs at breakfast . . . get a life! It's constant. But I wouldn't swap it for the world."

Like the majority of head coaches I've met, this international head coach believes that his empathic leadership style has a positive impact on his own wellbeing, due to sharing in more positive experiences than negative ones. Similarly, a cricket head coach said, "Most of the squad are not going through bad stuff; they are going through good stuff." Indeed, head coaches find their close relationships and sharing in the experiences of athletes an enjoyable part of their leadership. An international handball head coach told me, "I think it's one of the more fulfilling parts of coaching. If you're getting to know and understand them and you're helping them to achieve what they want to achieve, on or off the court; maybe they achieve things off the court it can be equally rewarding. The tough ones are injuries and things. You're not directly responsible, but you had them in the game at that point and you feel it, you know. But on the whole, it's more fulfilling than it is draining. It's rewarding."

However, leaders need to remain alert. There is always a danger that some will take advantage of an empathic approach and the close relationships they develop with a head coach. There is also a concern for the leader becoming biased towards athletes they have grown too close to.

Whether it's due to vicarious emotions or workload, maintaining an awareness of what the strains of leadership are doing to you is vital. Sometimes it takes someone else to notice when the burden is too much. This is where a mentor can be helpful. The head coach of a women's football team offers the following advice: "Make sure you have at least one mentor. I have a couple who are really good people, and they'll say to me,

'Look, you need to calm down,' or confirm that I'm doing the right thing, or ask if I've thought about it another way. It relieves some of the burden."

All of the head coaches that I've met in elite sport have mentors, and they have wisely chosen them themselves. An empathic leader who understands their own needs will be able to choose suitable mentors who can help to satisfy those needs through their mentorship. The head coach of a men's football team in Australasia told me, "I need someone to be empathic with *me*; a critical friend, who can be empathic and make you reflect when you need to. You need someone to vent to and someone who is honest and will disagree when you need it. Someone to lean on. I'm fortunate that I've got very good friends who are football people around me. I have my own mentors. I don't just have one, I have a few that I lean on, and it will be someone whose skill set suits the issue at hand. I think a lot of workplace practices have someone to go to and that's great, there is value to it, but if you have your own friend who does that, it goes a long way, believe me."

The pressures of leadership are certainly high in the context of elite sport and these pressures can increase due to unforeseen circumstances. Once again, only by being self-aware and practising self-empathy will you understand your own situation and needs. Sometimes a break will seem impossible, but remember you are no good to anyone without your own wellbeing. Getting away from your leadership role helps to prevent burnout and provides valuable time for reflection and revising goals. If it's not a holiday, time spent with family might help. We live in a time when we all seem to struggle with achieving a work/life balance. A men's football head coach explained: "It's extremely difficult. You have to have a very understanding wife. I guess for Pep (Guardiola) at his level, the money must make it easier. And he's taken a hiatus when he's been burned out. It does become your life. My little girl wants nothing to do with football, she won't touch a ball because she sees it as the thing that takes Daddy away. That's why it's extremely important for me to have the couple of hours spent here and there with her, my wife, for her and my wife and myself. It's extremely important. Oh, yeah, it's not easy. It is draining, it takes up every minute of every hour of every day. I have points where I have to completely switch off. I have my phone switched off and I'm with my wife and daughter, I spend the hours I need to just do something normal – go to the park, for a walk, the cinema, a meal with my wife – something normal where you can chill out and switch off, you know. Completely disconnect. It keeps your mind fresh, and you have family, and they are important, and they play an important part in you being successful."

Elite head coaches regret that getting the work/life balance right isn't always possible in a high-performance role and accept this as part of the job.

An international hockey head coach explained by saying, "My wife played high-level sport, so she has some empathy for it, you know, I'm lucky. I've spoken to other guys and their other halves lack the understanding and a lot of coaches I know are divorced. There's a coach I know, who is one of the best coaches in the world and he's getting divorced. I look at his situation and it's not surprising. I often thought, 'How are you balancing that?'"

As a leader of a team, you will face demands emanating from a variety of directions. There are the athletes, of course, and all the other stakeholders that come with the role. Then there's your family at home. Ultimately, it might be the wellbeing of the last person on your list that will determine the success of everything else: and too often that last person is you!

Managing Your Career

Self-empathy is also about understanding how behaviours and emotions may be rooted in personal history and career-related events.[18] To be an empathic leader, you need to understand where you've come from and how that influences where you are headed. In elite sport leadership, people often refer to whether or not you were a professional athlete before your coaching career. It remains unclear as to whether this is advantageous career wise,[19] but some believe such experience facilitates empathic ability.[20] Athletes seem to appreciate being understood and may feel this understanding is more likely if their head coach has had to perform in their shoes (an example of perceived empathy).

Specific experiences may well help you become a more empathic leader, as might age.[21] Your life experiences are practice for understanding the feelings of others in situations familiar to you.[22] This suggests that empathising for someone older may be more difficult,[23] and could present a problem for a young leader. However, a head coach in elite sport being younger than athletes is rare. It is also possible that too big an age gap dissolves empathy. Broadly speaking, older generations tend to show less understanding of the lives and habits of young people. Perhaps this explains why the most successful age range of head coaches is 44–60 years.[24]

Although many coaches plough on beyond these ages, sport leadership is certainly a tough career, arguably as tough as leadership in most other industries, which is highlighted by the average length of tenure. In European football, head coaches tend to come and go every few months. In England, the job with the highest turnover is chambermaid and the second is head coach at a football club, and almost half of those coaches who lose their positions don't acquire another position.[25]

Fresh challenges present themselves with each new job. An unfamiliar squad of athletes means a whole new set of emotions need to be understood. Of course, more competent leaders will move jobs less frequently, but the ability to adapt is paramount. Adapting to new situations is understood to be the most general and basic conceptualisation of competence.[26] Empathy can help a new head coach not only to adapt but also to understand if a situation will suit them and to devise an approach that best fits.[27]

With increased squad sizes and teams of support staff, sport leaders have a growing group of individuals to relate to. This may become a real test since in a group of 50 individuals, there are 1,225 one-on-one relationships, and numerous complex social combinations to get to grips with.[28] For a new leader, there is rarely enough time to meet everyone before the judgements begin.

Getting a new leader has enormous implications for athletes, who suddenly feel less secure. As the new head coach, you need to rapidly build trust, create bonds,[29] and enhance organisational connectedness.[30] Getting to know athletes is challenging enough, but it's a continuous process as young talent emerges and new signings arrive. You need to focus on each and every relationship in order to accurately hear the ideas and concerns of groups and individuals considered to be stakeholders. As well as the athletes, this includes the fans, the owners, governing bodies, training and medical staff, the local media, and the local community. Before considering a position, you need to believe you are the right fit and can align with these stakeholders. This requires both self-empathy and empathising with all stakeholders.

The fans will have expectations of their club that need to be understood and met.[31] This is likely to include style of play and even coach and athlete conduct, which can impact a club's reputation. An empathic leader's advantages include a moral compass,[32] which heightens sensitivity to both the needs of athletes and fans.[33] There is a danger in some industries of the customer and the organisation becoming disconnected.[34] Sport is unlikely to be immune from this danger. The distance between athletes and fans has grown in many ways. Athletes in the highest paid sports increasingly lead separate lives; their wealth, social power, and fame are likely to create distance and dilute their empathy for their fans.[35] As an empathic leader, these are some of the issues towards which you will need to demonstrate understanding.

The bigger the organisation, the more closely a new leader's behaviour will be observed. A demonstration of empathy and respect for other stakeholders will be noticed and enhance your reputation, increasing respect,[36] which enhances your influence over others. As an empathic head coach, you will have a greater awareness of yourself and your environment and, therefore, a better chance of remaining and succeeding in a new role and enjoying positive and long-term relationships.

According to the Greek philosopher Aristotle, knowing yourself is the beginning of all wisdom, and research shows there is a relationship between increased self-awareness and the kind of prosocial behaviours expected of empathic leadership.[37] Based on self-knowledge, as an empathic leader you will become a wise leader. Matters ignored within your own psychology will encourage defensive behaviours that inhibit empathic skills and leave you more vulnerable to the threat of vicariously felt negative emotions.[38] Through your efforts to understand yourself, you will not only improve your leadership, but you will also maintain your wellbeing and improve your decision making, as you become a stronger and more sustainable leader. However, it takes courage and commitment to grow self-knowledge, and there are no shortcuts.

Notes

1. Decety, J. & Lamm, C. (2007). The role of the right temporoparietal junction in social interaction: How low-level computational processes contribute to meta-cognition. *Neuroscientist, 13*(6), 580–593.
2. Decety, J. & Jackson, P. L. (2004). The functional architecture of human empathy. *Behavioral and Cognitive Neuroscience Reviews, 3*(2), 71–100.
3. Lanzoni, S. (2018). *Empathy: A history*. Yale University Press.
4. Niezink, L., & Train, K. (2020). The self in empathy: Self-empathy. *Psychology Today*. www.psychologytoday.com/gb/blog/empathic-intervision/202007/the-self-in-empathy-self-empathy
5. Wilson, T. D. *et al.* (2014). Just think: The challenges of the disengaged mind. *Science, 345*(6192), 75–77).
6. Mulhern, S. (2015). Can daydreaming improve my race time? *Running Magazine* https://runningmagazine.ca/sections/training/can-daydreaming-improve-my-race-time
7. Fries, A. (2009). *Daydreams at work: Wake up your creative powers*. Capital Books.
8. Baer, M., Dane, E. & Madrid, H. P. (2021). Zoning out or breaking through? Linking daydreaming to creativity in the workplace. *Academy of Management Journal, 64*(5), 1553–1577.
9. Jackson, S. A. (2000). Joy, fun, and flow state in sport. In In Y. L. Hanin (Ed.), *Emotions in sport* (pp. 135–155). Human Kinetics.
10. Longshore, K. & Sachs, M. (2015). Mindfulness training for coaches: A mixed-method exploratory study. *Journal of Clinical Sport* Psychology, *9*(2), 116–137.

11. Mandela, N. (2010). *Conversations with myself.* Macmillan, 2010.

12. Stengel, R. (2008). Mandela: His 8 lessons of leadership. *Time,* 9 July. https://content.time.com/time/subscriber/article/0,33009,1821659-2,00.html

13. Blum, C. A. (2014). Practicing self-care for nurses: A nursing program initiative. *Online Journal of Issues in Nursing, 19*(3). https://doi.org/10.3912/OJIN.Vol19No03Man03

14. Tracy, S. J. (2017). Burnout. In *The International Encyclopedia of Organizational Communication* (pp. 1–9). John Wiley & Sons. doi:10.1002/9781118955567.wbieoc015

15. Antonakis, J. (2004). On why "emotional intelligence" will not predict leadership effectiveness beyond iq or the "big five": An extension and rejoinder. *Organizational Analysis, 12*(2), 171–182

16. Batson, C., Ahmad, N. & Stocks, (2004), Benefits and liabilities of empathy-induced altruism. In A. G. Miller (Ed.), The social psychology of good and evil (pp. 359–385). Guilford Press.

17. Sloman, R., Rosen, G., Rom, M. & Shir, Y. (2005). Nurses' assessment of pain in surgical patients. *Journal of Advanced Nursing, 52*(2), 125–132.

18. Moore, B. E. & Fine, B. D. (1990). *Psychoanalytic terms and concepts.* American Psychoanalytic Association.

19. Peachey, J. W., Zhou, Y., Damon, Z. J. & Burton, L. J. (2015). Forty Years of leadership research in sport management: A review, synthesis, and conceptual framework. *Journal of Sport Management, 29*(5), 570–587.

20. Kock, N., Mayfield, M., Mayfield, J., Sexton, S. & De La Garza, L. M. (2019). Empathetic leadership: How leader emotional support and understanding influences follower performance. *Journal of Leadership and Organizational Studies, 26*(2), 217–236.

21. Sze, J. A., Gyurak, A., Goodkind, M. S. & Levenson, R. W. (2012). Greater emotional empathy and prosocial behavior in late life. *Emotion, 12*(5), 1129–1140.

22. Lorimer, R. & Jowett, S. (2009). Empathic accuracy in coach–athlete dyads who participate in team and individual sports. *Psychology of Sport and Exercise, 10*(1), 152–158.

23. Katz, L. K. (1963). *Empathy: Its nature and uses.* Free Press of Glencoe.

24. Njuguna, C. (2022). Top 10 of the best young football managers 2022: Global ranking SportsBrief.com. https://sportsbrief.com/facts/top-listicles/13829-top-10-young-football-managers-2022-global-ranking

25. Ancelotti, C., Brady, C. & Forde, M. (2017). *Quiet leadership.* Portfolio/Penguin.

26. Spitzberg, B. H. & Cupach, W. R. (1984). *Interpersonal communication competence.* Sage Publications.

27. O'Neil, D. A. The Value of Emotional Intelligence for High Performance Coaching: A Commentary. *Int. J. Sports Sci. Coach.* **6**, (2011).

28. Harari, Y. N. (2011). *Sapiens: A brief history of humankind.* Random House.

29. Tzouramani, E. L (2017). Leadership and empathy. In J. Marques & S. Dhiman (Eds), *Leadership today: Practices for personal and professional development* (pp. 197–216). Springer. doi:10.1007/978-3-319-31036-7_11

30. Pavlovich, K. & Krahnke, K. (2012). Empathy, connectedness and organisation. *Journal of Business Ethics, 105*, 131–137.

31. Van Tonder, C. L. & Berner, A. (2003). The postmodern consumer: Implications of changing customer expectations for organisation development in service organisations. *SA Journal of Industrial Psychology, 29*(3), 1–10.

32. Lennick, D. & Kiel, F. (2011). *Moral intelligence 2.0: Enhancing business performance and leadership success in turbulent times*. Prentice Hall.

33. Pavlovich, K. & Krahnke, K. (2013). *Organizing through empathy*. Routledge.

34. Peppard, J. (2000). Customer relationship management (CRM) in financial services. *European Management Journal, 18*(3), 312–327.

35. Sherman, G. D., Lerner, J. S., Renshon, J., Ma-Kellams, C. & Joel, S. (2015). Perceiving others' feelings. *Social Psychological and Personality Science, 6*, 559–569.

36. Marques, J. (2015). The changed leadership landscape: What matters today. *Journal of Management Development, 34*(10), 1310–1322.

37. Pate, L. & Shoblom, T. L. (2013). The ACES decision-making technique as a reframing tool for increasing empathy. In K. Pavlovich & K. Krahnke (Eds), *Organizing through empathy* (pp. 142–157). Routledge.

38. Kisfalvi, V. (2013). Working through the past: How personal history influences leaders' emotions and capacity for empathy. In K. Pavlovich & K. Krahnke (Eds), *Organizing through empathy* (pp. 75–92). Routledge.

Empathic Communication

2

While communication is possible without empathy, a non-empathic communicator will be less effective as a leader. Empathic communication requires understanding, compassion, and consideration for the feelings and opinions of others.[1] It leads to trust and openness, and it reduces negative behaviours such as backstabbing and scheming. By knowing the other, communication can be tailored more appropriately. The knowledge you have of others needs to be accurate and current. This is achieved through regular communication. Being strangers just encourages misunderstandings, which brings chaos and causes relationship breakdown. As a leader becomes aware of a follower's needs, they can express this awareness through further communications.[2] As mutual understanding evolves, so will the clarity and effectiveness of communication, enhancing alignment, and performance.

Dynamic Communication

Empathic communication is not a momentary phenomenon; it must endure. Empathy thrives on a regular back and forth – what is often referred to as *dynamic communication*.[3] As an empathic leader, you should maintain curiosity, with the primary aim of gaining deeper understanding.[4] Empathy has to be a process, with feedback and regular adjustments. Dynamic communication also helps to limit the negative influence of *power* on empathy and mutual understanding.[3]

This consequence of power should not be underestimated. Studies have shown that a leader's *empathic accuracy* (use of empathy in efforts to

DOI: 10.4324/9781003324676-3

accurately predict the behaviour and emotions of others[5, 6]) is lower for those with more structural power.[7] Power's dilution of empathy has been apparent to psychologists since Zimbardo's Stanford Prison Guard studies in the early 1970s,[8] which demonstrated the potential for those with power to dehumanise those they rule over.[9] As long as empathic communication is maintained, you shouldn't have to worry about dehumanising your athletes. This may sound extreme, but it is worth remembering that just a couple of decades ago there were head coaches working in elite sport who viewed their athletes as little more than shirt numbers.

In previous eras, some head coaches had the attitude that they had coached all types of personalities and had *seen it all*. Such hubris leads to incorrect assumptions and, therefore, poor decision making.[10] People are always evolving and will change significantly throughout a sporting career. Expectations of athletes will be inflexible if coaches base them on assessments made at the beginning of a season or when they were recruited.[11] An empathic leader will have the latest data.

As well as its positive impact on cognition and understanding, dynamic communication also encourages a dynamic attunement of emotions across a group.[4, 12, 13] This further enhances alignment and cohesion, and will improve the working climate. With a focus on listening and understanding, cooperative relationships will develop, allowing your teams to gel and thrive.[14]

Head coaches working in elite sport today stress the importance of using every opportunity to update their knowledge and understanding of each athlete. A men's football head coach told me, "Sometimes I'll chat with younger players while they're out on a training pitch juggling the ball, as I know they feel more comfortable that way." This flexibility in communication may have been mastered by a handful of coaches in the latter decades of the last century, but it has become commonplace and expected, as this hockey head coach explains: "There was very little of these kinds of conversations. It was a lot more distant and direct when I started coaching 20 years ago. I just think athletes don't respond to distant, direct, and dictatorial anymore."

These conversations between leader and athlete become expected and natural. They make the athlete feel relevant and that they matter.[15] *Mattering* has become strongly associated with human wellbeing and performance,[16] and so should be relevant to any leader with ambition. It is important that the athlete feels not only that they matter, but that their opinions and ideas do too. Where once athletes weren't consulted, they are now consulted regularly. But it is no good talking with athletes during a warm-up if you're not taking in what they are saying. An empathic leader will ensure athletes know they are being heard.

The communicative priority for an empathic leader is listening, and this has to include more than what is explicitly conveyed.[17] The more you get to know people, the easier it becomes to understand what their body language means. Body language and facial expressions should be viewed as further sources of knowledge and understanding. This is another example of the empathic leader's skills of data collection, but it can work both ways. Empathic head coaches understand that the athletes are watching them all the time. What the athletes see has an impact. It may not always be obvious to the head coach what they themselves are communicating. They may be revealing their emotions to their athletes, and this could prove detrimental to performance. Although authenticity is important, a nervous head coach won't want to spread those nerves to their athletes. A football head coach, working in Scandinavia, told me, "I consider this a lot, my body language, my temperament. I think a lot of coaches should consider this." This is clearly something that leaders have to work on: "I have always been aware of it; it doesn't mean I get it right all of the time." And circumstances can make things more difficult: "Yes, especially now coming to a new country this winter and having to coach in English. I have a new squad and I must consider how things look to them."

During competition, athletes are typically further from their leader, and often this means body language is all they have to understand how their leader is feeling. It's not only the athletes on the field of play who need to be considered, as another football head coach explains: "I shout a lot and talk to the other coaches a lot, and I forget there are players on the bench too and they are listening. So I have to take care of my choice of words and my body language."

An empathic leader comes to understand that the emotions they display will have an impact on those they lead. In time, a leader can learn to control their displays of emotion and sometimes even choose to display emotions strategically. Dynamic communication helps a leader to monitor how their own body language and words influence athletes. Any head coach can learn how they need to improve and work on that. This is another example of the importance of listening to those you lead. It can help you develop into a better leader who has a greater influence on the team.

In sport, listening is particularly important when it comes to understanding issues influencing wellbeing. This doesn't only facilitate giving the appropriate support but also allows informed decisions to be made concerning things like selection and substitutions. "If we don't listen, we won't find ways forward," a head coach of a women's football team told me. *"Guessing what they are thinking or what they're going through is no good."*

When not talking themselves, leaders can often be guilty of waiting to reply rather than focusing on listening. The aim can be to win the conversation without realising knowledge can be missed out on. It's an easy trap to fall into, since society has become dominated by this focus on winning conversations rather than learning from others. It's a trend that demolishes human relations, which will be disastrous at home, in social settings, and certainly in leadership. A leader who has the intention to understand isn't focused on conquering discussions or demonstrating their power in relationships. Listening is inherent in empathic communication. A good listener will treat a speaker without judgement and with acceptance. A true listener is someone who gains understanding and empathises with what is being said.

A crucial part of the listening process is that the response ensures the athlete knows that they have been heard.[18] Listening can have huge consequences for the culture and climate of an elite environment.[19] The knowledge and understanding gained by a leader enhances the clarity of future communications. The alternative is that a leader exposes him- or herself to misunderstanding, misconceptions, and miscommunications.

Miscommunications

Miscommunications, misconceptions, and misunderstandings are wonderful ingredients for entertainment. They are guaranteed to create chaos. Whether it's a Shakespeare play, a Hollywood romcom, or a situation comedy on TV, a misunderstanding can be the seed of humour. In leadership, however, misunderstandings and chaos are to be avoided.

In professional sport, misunderstandings lead to poor performances and bad results. They can ruin relationships and end careers. Elite sport is a mix of cultures, accents, and ages. Athletes and coaches are drawn from a diversity of backgrounds, which makes focusing on clarity of communication more vital.

Empathic leaders carefully reflect on what they say and what they hear. They take into consideration the person they are talking with and the context in which the conversation is taking place. The term *culturally cognizant listening* has been employed to describe a non-judgemental, active listening style with self-reflection and perspective-taking behaviours, like empathy.[20] For example, it is crucial that head coaches fully understand a situation before they speak to athletes or a whole group.[21] The aim for any leader has to be congruence between both sides of a conversation. Not just in words, but in thoughts. This is referred to as *listening fidelity*,[22] which should be a leader's aim. More simply put, this is when a message is heard as a speaker intends it to be heard.

It is important that leaders consider the kind of language they use. In elite sport, a head coach will usually have a wealth of experience and education on his specialist subject. As well as cultural differences, there may be varied levels of educational background within the team. A head coach may have been educated to a higher level than some of their young athletes in particular, and will no doubt have attended a multitude of coaching courses where technical language becomes the norm. This may mean head coaches use words that their athletes do not recognise. There is a lack of research on the use of appropriate language for communicating while coaching; however, information that needs to be given to an athlete needs to be given in a way in which it is best understood. This is no doubt true in other industries. Leaders are, by definition, likely to be more experienced, and this will influence the vocabulary they use. Failing to be understood will cause problems for a leader in all contexts. The likelihood of problems is increased when a leader is new to a role and unfamiliar to the team.

An interesting situation was described to me by one head coach, who learned that the intended message of a new coach can easily be misunderstood: "A group of female athletes came to me and said, 'Look, we don't like the way you shout at us all of the time.' And firstly, it's good because they obviously felt comfortable in coming to talk to me. But it kind of caught me off guard. I looked at my assistant coach in disbelief and he was smiling. Then the girls saw him, and they looked as confused as I did. I asked him what was funny, and he explained that having known me for years, he knew that I never shouted at them, but he also explained that he knew why they thought I was shouting. It was my accent and the way I talk. I'm from Glasgow and we can sound a bit aggressive in natural conversation if you don't know us."

Reflecting on this incident, the head coach saw it as an opportunity to learn and grow: "I learned to have more self-awareness, understand who I am. I'm a dry-humoured Glaswegian and can't be anyone else." This enabled the coach to move forward positively after what had been a negative moment:""Once we got that out of the way, the girls were less apprehensive about me. Sometimes when I gave instructions, they smiled, and I realised this meant that I was sounding like I was shouting or being overly aggressive. So we both learned." Once mutual understanding becomes apparent it becomes easier for a leader to tailor communication appropriately.

The head coach of a football team described to me an example of understanding an individual athlete and then tailoring communication appropriately: "A player was scouted, he had obvious talents, moving quickly through the ranks, but at the same time was immature in a lot of ways, specifically psychologically for his age. He was being discussed and assessed and moving through the system like an adult, but with a child's brain. So, when we sat down with him, we needed to understand from him what his competence level was for taking information in and what were the realities of that. We had to dumb it down, for want of a better term. We decided I had to deliver a message in a way that would have been suitable for a Grade 12 child, rather than a seasoned professional who has other stuff in his life like family and finance. This was basically a raw kid who was just playing a game and all the other things going on in his brain he just wasn't ready for, so we had to really bring it down and explain to him carefully what we wanted from him."

The most important consideration is that the message is received as the sender of that message intends it to be received. Edwin Rutsch, the Founding Director of the Center for Building a Culture of Empathy, suggests an approach he describes as *mutual active listening*. The process increases mutual understanding by ensuring that each person feels fully heard to their satisfaction. In his *empathy circles*, participants convey the message they've heard and describe how they've understood it. This can be time-consuming, but in professional settings it ensures congruence and listening fidelity. Sometimes communication has to be prioritised over time, but all contexts have their own requirements.

Tailoring Communication

Empathic leaders communicate skilfully by tailoring communication for individuals and for contexts. There are certain situations in leadership where the style of communication is considered crucial.[10, 23] In elite sport, these situations include directing instructions on to the field of play, giving feedback, and, of course, announcing team selection. Empathic leaders use everything they know to understand how information will be received, but in the turmoil of competitive action, this is always going to be challenging.

Empathic leadership is inhibited by distance,[2] and so communicating with athletes from the distance of the touchline is likely to be challenging. The approach will not be the same for all athletes, and so the leader needs to know and understand each individual in the squad. Some will respond to an emotional or aggressive instruction, others to calmness and encouragement.

The empathic leader will tailor communication, such as the delivery of instructions, to each individual.[24] A head coach from North America explained to me that delivering instructions depends on knowing the person you are speaking to: "I know there are certain players that need certain deliveries of a message. It depends on what sort of person they are." This focus on the uniqueness of athletes and their needs was not always common in sport leadership as a rugby union head coach confirmed: "Back when I was playing, delivery of instructions was carried out in a one-size-fits-all way." It's not just athlete individuality that needs to be considered.

When communicating during the heat of action, a head coach needs to take into consideration a multitude of variables: the venue, the noise levels, the score, and who is listening. Understanding what each listener can do with the information communicated is just as important as understanding how the athlete will receive it. This will include officials, fans, and, of course, the opposition.

It is also important for the head coach to consider how they are feeling and understand their own character traits, as this too can influence their communications. Coaches who feel uncomfortable being critical may avoid doing so out of fear of unfavourable reactions, but there are moments when criticism is exactly what is required.[25] The head coach also needs to be aware of their own biases or stereotypes that might block the intake of new information with unconscious assumptions.[26] A personal reaction to a defeat may affect communication with athletes and then, in turn, threaten a relationship.[27] Achieving this awareness requires leaders to constantly question themselves, not just their athletes.

Head coaches may provide regular directions to help their athletes.[28] When athletes feel that directions have been conveyed empathically, it will have a positive influence on their emotional reaction and, therefore, their performance.[29] Displays of empathic concern have been shown to reduce negative affect, such as loss of confidence.[30]

An empathic leader understands that it is also important for athletes to treat each other as individuals with different needs. A head coach working in New Zealand told me how important it is for athletes to understand the impact their words can have on others, particularly in emotional moments: "We brought in a mental skills coach, more specifically to develop clarity of communication on the pitch." It wasn't only pitch time that this coach was concerned about: "When the players enter the changing rooms at half time, they have a few minutes for breathing exercises and to calm down before we deliver the messages, and we also do mindfulness at training." When I asked what impact this has had, the coach told me, "It's helped bind the group together this season." He went on to say that his aim is to "encourage open communication and honesty between players and try to make them aware of the importance of considering the tone and emotion behind a communication". Our emotions can get the better of us, particularly when we feel a colleague has let us down: "We need to realise that nobody wants to make a mistake." It is certainly going to make things worse if a mistake on the field is followed by mistakes off it. The athletes should come to appreciate that these strategies are helping them to develop too.

The head coaches I have spoken with assure me that information is constantly sought by modern athletes, and so they don't tend to become annoyed at receiving it. The head coach of a women's football team told me, "It's just a matter of explaining why and getting the delivery right. Players today are hungry for information, it's not like it was when I played." The head coach of an international rugby union team agreed and stressed how little athletes like uncertainty: "Uncertainty is a derailer for a lot of them and they need to know what's going on, and once you find out who they are, you can give them a heads up and it helps them massively. They like clarity, as well as being understood."

It's not always the case that the leader has answers, but they might lie close by. As well as a team of staff, head coaches are surrounded by competent professionals with their own ideas, which can be drawn on by any leader willing to listen. This is certainly applicable when developing strategies for communication that impact the athletes themselves. Their views should be sought and valued.

An empathic communicator is said to communicate using choices instead of demands.[31] This policy is evident in elite sport where the values of offering choices and maintaining clarity in communication are clearly recognised.[18] In order to avoid uncertainty and misunderstandings, head coaches prefer face-to-face communication where possible. However, to accommodate individual preferences, more and more communication methods are influenced by athletes. How they prefer to receive feedback from the head coach is a good example.

Empathic leaders are expected to provide regular feedback,[28] but they may feel uncomfortable if what they have to say is negative, possibly due to their inherent understanding of how this will impact the athlete.[25] The cushion for negative feedback lies in the empathy itself. Researchers have found that when it is obvious that a leader is being empathic, it reduces any negative affect.[30] Just by listening and reforming methods of feedback, the head coach is displaying empathy. A female head coach of a women's team told me that having the athletes influence the way feedback is provided "makes for a better environment. They all decided that to have it in small groups was better. So that was player led." However, a group of any size has its own dynamics.

It is important that group feedback sessions are not dominated by the same people. The voice of the least confident can be lost. A head coach working in Australia suggested that this can be overcome "by having feedback in very small groups or individually, if it's not working in a larger group. That's what we did last season, after a bad spell."

An international rugby union coach explained to me that once the athletes become familiar, it is possible to use one or two as a barometer for certain things: "When I was at one club, I had a player who was my barometer. If he came to me and said he was tired. I'd say, 'Oh shit! We must be over training them because this guy will train until his body fails.' But if another player came to me and said, 'I'm tired,' and he was someone I knew who just didn't like training, I'd say get on with it."

This approach is only made possible by an in-depth knowledge of each athlete and time for reflection before action.

Reflection before reaction is a common response when you ask head coaches in elite sport about anything – particularly if it's regarding something that comes out of nowhere. An international volleyball head coach told me that he needs to buy time sometimes to reflect on situations and offered the following example: "A player said he's going to leave at the end of the season. I said: 'well, hang on a minute, tell me why and then let me give it some thought.' And I thought about it overnight, slept on it, if you like, and then had a better conversation with him the following day."

I asked the head coach why he did this exactly. He said that "it's about not having that emotional reaction in the moment and rationalising your response". An experienced head coach of a netball team added that a leader has to have an awareness of the athletes' need for reflection time: "I don't rip into them after the game; they need time to reflect and so do I. Then you can both make a rational reaction." This is the kind of philosophy that a leader needs to maintain high-quality relationships during moments of disappointment or chaos.

Modes of Communication

A dilemma currently facing leaders, if not all of us, is choosing the best methods of communication for each situation. So many are available, and it seems to be growing every day with an infinite number of apps, as well as the standard text, phone call, email, video call, and face-to-face interaction. A handball head coach told me, "I give players a choice of how they want to be notified about selection. Maybe that wouldn't have been the case 20 years ago." The question we must ask in each situation is which of these modes of communication best maintains what a leader is after: congruence, listening fidelity, empathic understanding, and perceived empathy.

There are bound to be generational differences in the preferences expressed by athletes, but they are not the only demographic distinctions. An international rugby union head coach told me that "the men want information given face to face, but the women I coach told me they prefer everything by email". The head coach of a women's football team agreed: "Women like a record of what you've said; blokes don't care so much about that stuff."

In elite sport, some leaders have developed their own rules concerning which mode of communication to use for what, with texting, for example, being acceptable for the more benign messages. A cricket coach told me that he employs text messaging for "logistics: time, kits to wear. Everything else is face to face. If I phone, I use Facetime (video call). I'll send a *well done* via text, but anything we need to talk about it will be Facetime or in person." An ice hockey head coach also told me that he repeatedly tells his players that while logistical information may be sent out via text or email, all other communication between him and the players should take place face to face whenever possible.

Electronic communiques have their advantages. They provide a record or proof of a message, which leaves athletes without excuses for missing meetings. A head coach can see if the message has been read and soon get a reply if there's a problem. Text messaging can save a leader a great deal of time. A netball head coach told me that she asks her athletes to inform her when they are not going to be at training and for whatever reason, via text. If this was done via a phone call, it would interrupt the coach's preparation or journey, and the rest of the squad would suffer. It also provides a leader with time to replan training sessions, taking into consideration the latest absentees.

Despite the convenience and acceptance of a range of methods, face-to-face communication is considered the best way of avoiding misunderstandings in conversations, and head coaches often insist on it. Face-to-face communications allow the head coach to collect extra information. An international lacrosse head coach said that "it's an opportunity to assess body language". Such cues are important for empathic accuracy.[32] A netball head coach told me that she sees it as "an opportunity to gauge an individual's feelings and emotions unlike an email which shows no emotion". This shows how face-to-face communications allow empathic leaders to increase their knowledge of those they lead, and keep that knowledge up to date using physical, and psychological impression cues.[33]

Face-to-face meetings also provide an opportunity for head coaches to display empathy. A head coach in Australia said that "face-to-face shows not only empathy but also trust and support if communicated well". Expressing empathy can be done with no more than a raised eyebrow or a smile. This is impossible to achieve via email, and any display of empathy perceived by the athlete will have a positive influence on them.[29]

A men's football head coach said that he insists on his communication policies so that the athletes know where they are: "I prefer face to face. Sometimes they'll text me about something important and I respond saying I will not talk about this with you via text. Because the problem is how do they perceive me to have written something. If I write something, my tone, my voice, and how I present it depends more on how you feel at the time rather than how I mean it. Emojis arguably could help express emotions, but for me it has to be face-to-face conversation."

Emojis don't always help. To use them successfully, a leader needs to be certain about how they are perceived. A head coach of a women's football team told me that she used to use the upside-down smiley face quite a bit, but then "one of the players got me after training one day and said, 'You realise that means sarcasm?' I just thought it was a smiley face upside-down!" But even face-to-face messages can be misinterpreted.

An international volleyball head coach described a mistake he made early in his career when he told his athletes that he only cared about what they did at training and in matches, and that what went on in between was none of his business. It was reported back to him that he'd been entirely misunderstood: "I meant that if they want to go out socialising or whatever, they should do so. They took it as I didn't care about them and their personal lives and that they shouldn't come to me if they have problems. That's a huge difference. And that was face to face!"

Although face-to-face communication is preferred by all of the head coaches I've spoken to, an individual athlete may have good reason to dislike this method. They may feel a need to have a discussion with the head coach about their reason for not attending training. In such circumstances, care needs to be taken by the head coach to ensure that the needs of the group are met, without the individual athlete feeling ignored or unvalued.

Another situation that may lead an athlete to feel unvalued, or that they don't matter, is when they are left out of a team or squad. An international lacrosse head coach told me that a truly empathic leader should "discuss with the players how they would like to receive the news about team selection". A rugby union head coach added that "it is important for the coach to be available to communicate with non-selected players. Perhaps after the first training session post-game." This highlights how chosen policies can impact those athletes selected and those not selected. The perspectives of all athletes need to be taken into consideration. Arguably, in the short term anyway, the needs of the athletes selected are paramount. However, the negative impact on an athlete not selected may damage the relationship with the head coach and have negative consequences for the team over the longer term.

Empathic leaders are considered skilled communicators, capable of a variety of communication methods.[34] Embracing different modes of communication to meet the needs of athletes reflects an empathic leadership style. It hasn't always been like this in elite sport, as this experienced football head coach remembers: "The women's team, 20 years ago, when they picked a team, their players would have a time to phone the front office. Just a time slot, you know, and the receptionist women would say, you're in or you're out! And then if you're out, you could decide if you want a follow up call with the coach."

Another football head coach compared the situation with how things were when he was an athlete: "When I played in England, the Friday after training, bang: the manager stuck the starting team up on the wall and disappeared. I'm sure that still happens in some places." I said that having spoken to many head coaches about this, I would be surprised. He added something else that focuses on the athlete's perspective: "The crazy one for me is the manager naming a team an hour before kick-off. I mean, that would be bizarre to me. How does a player prepare? Secondly, if you name it before a game and one or two who are left out get really upset, you don't get any time, and that can impact the whole dressing room, an hour before kick-off instead of a day before, when it can be all done and dusted. I've never understood it." Once again, the long-term relationship between player and head coach is put at risk by this policy. In sport and any area of life, relationships matter.

In summary, empathic communication is a major component of the empathic leader's tool kit. Clarity and congruence will not only determine the impact of each communication but also the quality of relationships. Miscommunications are the enemy of leadership and will eventually lead to relationship breakdown, poor performance, and the downfall of the leader. Each context and individual requires a different approach, often a different mode of delivery. Understanding contexts comes with experience.

Understanding individuals comes through dynamic communication, close relationships, and empathy.

Notes

1. Williams, J. H. (2006). Improving safety communication skills: Becoming an empathic communicator. In *ASSE Professional Development Conference and Exposition 2006*. American Society of Safety Engineers (ASSE).
2. Kock, N., Mayfield, M., Mayfield, J., Sexton, S. & De La Garza, L. M. (2019). Empathetic leadership: How leader emotional support and understanding influences follower performance. *Journal of Leadership and Organizational Studies*, 26(2), 217–236.
3. Main, A., Walle, E. A., Kho, C. & Halpern, J. (2017). The interpersonal functions of empathy: A relational perspective. *Emotion Review*, 9(4), 358–366.
4. Halpern, J. (2001). *From detached concern to empathy: Humanizing medical practice*. Oxford University Press.
5. Ickes, W. (1993). Empathic accuracy. *Journal of Personality*, 61(4), 587–610.
6. Ickes, W. J. (1997). *Empathic accuracy*. Guilford Press.
7. Sherman, G. D., Lerner, J. S., Renshon, J., Ma-Kellams, C. & Joel, S. (2015). Perceiving others' feelings: The importance of personality and social structure. *Social Psychological and Personality Science*, 6(5), 559–569.
8. Zimbardo, P. G. (1971). The Power and Pathology of Imprisonment: Statement of Philip G. Zimbardo. Hearings before Subcommittee no. 3 of the Committee on the Judiciary, House of Representatives, 92nd Congress, 1st Session on Corrections Part II, Prisons. Prison Reform, and Prisoners' Rights, California. U.S. Government Printing Office.
9. Keltner, D., Gruenfeld, D. H. & Anderson, C. (2003). Power, approach, and inhibition. *Psychological Review*, 110(2), 265–284.
10. Lorimer, R. & Jowett, S. (2010). Feedback of information in the empathic accuracy of sport coaches. *Psychology of Sport and Exercise*, 11(1), 12–17.
11. Solomon, G. B., Golden, A. J., Ciapponi, T. M. & Martin, A. D. (1998). Coach expectations and differential feedback: Perceptual flexibility revisited. *Journal of Sport Behavior*, 21(3), 298–310.
12. Hollan, D. & Throop, C. J. (2008). Whatever happened to empathy? Introduction. *Ethos*, 36(4), 385–401.
13. Kupetz, M. (2014). Empathy displays as interactional achievements – Multimodal and sequential aspects. *Journal of Pragmatics*, 61, 4–34.
14. Mahsud, R., Yukl, G. & Prussia, G. (2010). Leader empathy, ethical leadership, and relations-oriented behaviors as antecedents of leader-member exchange quality. *Journal of Managerial Psychology*, 25(6), 561–577.

15. Ghaye, T., Allen, L. & Clark, N. (2021). The holistic wellbeing of elite youth performers: U MATTER. In N. Campbell, A. Brady & A. Tincknell-Smith (Eds), *Developing and supporting athlete wellbeing: Person first, athlete second* (pp. 18–32). Routledge.
16. Flett, G. (2018). *The psychology of mattering: Understanding the human need to be significant.* Elsevier Science.
17. Johnson, W. (1951). The spoken word and the great unsaid. *Quarterly Journal of Speech, 37,* 419–429.
18. Rollnick, S., Fader, J. S., Breckon, J. & Moyers, T. B. (2019). *Coaching athletes to be their best: Motivational interviewing in sports.* Guilford Press.
19. Parks, E. S. (2015). Listening with empathy in organizational communication. *Organization Development Journal, 33*(3), 9–22.
20. Landry-Meyer, L. (2021). Culturally cognizant listening. *International Journal of Listening.* https://doi.org/10.1080/10904018.2021.1964365
21. Bennett, M. J. (2001). *The empathic healer: An endangered species?* Academic Press.
22. Mulanax, A. & Powers, W. G. (2012). Listening fidelity development and relationship to receiver apprehension and locus of control. *International Journal of Listening, 15*(1), 69–78. https://doi.org/10.1080/10904018.2001.10499045
23. Stanger, N., Kavussanu, M. & Ring, C. (2012). Put yourself in their boots: Effects of empathy on emotion and aggression. *Journal of Sport and Exercise Psychology, 34*(2), 208–222.
24. Stajkovic, A. D. & Luthans, F. (1998). Self-efficacy and work-related performance: A meta-analysis. *Psychological Bulletin, 124*(2), 240–261.
25. Moss, S. E. & Sanchez, J. I. (2004). Are your employees avoiding you? Managerial strategies for closing the feedback gap. *Academy of Management Executive, 18*(1), 32–46.
26. Lorimer, R. (2013). The development of empathic accuracy in sports coaches. *Journal of Sport Psychology in Action, 4*(1), 26–33.
27. Lynch, J. (2001). *Creative coaching.* Human Kinetics.
28. London, M. & Smither, J. W. (2002). Feedback orientation, feedback culture, and the longitudinal performance management process. *Human Resource Management* Review, *12*(1), 81–100.
29. O'Malley, A. L. & Gregory, J. B. (2011). Don't be such a downer: Using positive psychology to enhance the value of negative feedback. *The Psychologist-Manager Journal, 14*(4), 247–264.
30. Young, S. F., Richard, E. M., Moukarzel, R. G., Steelman, L. A. & Gentry, W. A. (2017). How empathic concern helps leaders in providing negative feedback: A two study examination. *Journal of Occupational and Organizational Psychology, 90*(4), 535–558.

31. Williams, J. H. (2006, June). Improving safety communication skills: Becoming an empathic communicator [Conference presentation]. ASSE Professional Development Conference and Exposition, Seattle, WA, United States.
32. Lorimer, R. & Jowett, S. (2009). Empathic accuracy in coach–athlete dyads who participate in team and individual sports. *Psychology of Sport and Exercise, 10*(1), 152–158.
33. Solomon, G. & Lobinger, B. (2011). Sources of expectancy information among coaches: A cross cultural investigation. *Theories and Applications, 1*(1), 46–57.
34. Socas, J. (2018). Empathy: The key ingredient for better leadership. *International Leadership Journal, 10,* 97–110.

Empathic Relationships   **3**

Failing to establish relationships or experiencing relationship breakdown usually spells the end for a leader in any industry. Empathic leaders enjoy a closer relationship with those they lead. The empathic leader's quest for closer relationships is aided by current societal expectations for employees to have a closer relationship with their leaders.[1] A closer relationship between a leader and a team member encourages greater knowledge and understanding of each other. This enhances empathic accuracy, reducing the likelihood of unexpected behaviour or reactions to situations. For an empathic leader, the knowledge and understanding of another informs decision making, which will improve performance, whatever the context.[2] It also allows a leader's instructions and feedback to be tailored appropriately, with respect to contexts and emotional states, reducing uncertainty and ensuring instructions are clear for team members.[3] However, it is not always easy for a leader to ensure relationships with team members are close. The emotionally volatile environments of elite sport make this challenging, and the technology of this era has added new obstacles.

In E. M. Forster's novel *Howards End*, one of the main characters is a cold industrial leader called Henry Wilcox. Through Wilcox, Forster expressed his concerns about the direction in which leadership was travelling in the early twentieth century. Henry lacks empathy for his workers and, consequently, has a distant relationship with them. In one scene, Wilcox highlights his flaw: "I look at the faces of the clerks in my own office, and observe them to be dull, but I don't know what's going on beneath."

An empathic leader creates emotional bonds and enjoys closer relationships than were absent in previous eras.[4, 5] The head coach of a cricket team described the leader he had 20 years ago when he was a player,

DOI: 10.4324/9781003324676-4

as a distant figure, noting: "The coach facilitated some stuff in the morning, some catching or something, and that was it. He picked a team, there was no communication about how we were going to approach it. At lunch when the players came off, they'd get together as a group and discuss. So, right, we need to do this better; the coach might be having lunch or alone in a corner, ha ha! It was so different." An international lacrosse head coach told me that his role "is now about relationships, whereas previously they believed it was about passing on knowledge. That's a change I've seen on my coaching journey. My feeling is that as a younger less experienced coach, coaching was about imparting knowledge, about being the sage on the stage. It was to be the person who told the athlete what to do and then they went out there and did it the best they could. Or someone who told the team what they were to do, and they go and attempt to do that at a team level. Now it's about relationships and understanding."

A European ice hockey head coach described how his relationship with team members is more relaxed today than things may have been in the previous eras, and that this plays out in the language used: "In our language, we talk differently to older people than to younger people, you use different endings to the words. You don't do that in English. But many coaches say they don't let them use that closer language. These formal things they think are important. I don't agree. I don't mind players calling me by my nickname once in a while."

Around the same time as Forster wrote *Howards End*, he penned a dystopian novella, *The Machine*, in which human beings live in pods and lack physical face-to-face contact, only ever seeing other faces on screens.

A hundred years on, thankfully, there are fewer Henry Wilcoxes around. However, Forster's fears about social interaction seem even more pressing. Societal changes brought about by technological advances have transformed the relationship playing field. Social media researchers have already discovered that physical distancing is influencing adolescent neural development,[6] and now virtual worlds are beginning to evolve. Where will that take us? Head coaches in elite sport are rising to this challenge by insisting on face-to-face contact wherever possible. "Without regular face-to-face conversations and physical contact, how will I ever become close to my players?" an international handball head coach asked me.

A women's football head coach told me, "I've had young girls join us who are so used to communicating on their devices that they struggle to look me in the eye, and that's worrying; it has to change if we are going to have a relationship." Other head coaches agreed that they must put in work to develop human qualities that are missing in young people, who are not as used to socialising face to face as previous generations.

The head coach of a men's football team told me that close relationships bring the kind of understanding that can make words unnecessary: "We create that environment where the players will know without me saying anything. From my body language or something maybe." He explained that this works both ways: "I've had players turn up for training and are not performing well, the body language has changed, and I know that there must be things going on in the background and being aware of them helps."

Some head coaches mentioned the use of psychological profiling, as a kind of shortcut to getting to know players. However, knowing someone by looking at data on a screen is not enough. An international rugby union head coach told me that it's about getting to know them on a human level, and that this takes time: "The more time, the more you get to know them – it's as simple as that really. Sometimes it's taken me two years to really understand a player."

With larger squads than ever before, head coaches need more time than ever before to get to know their athletes. A football head coach in Scandinavia told me, "I arrive first at training every day. And I'm last to leave, too. This is easier right now because I'm in another country and have no family or social life here, I'm here to work. I don't need to go home. I try to be available to players for all the informal chats you have; I think that's the best way to get to know them and show I care."

Gaining knowledge of individuals is paramount.[7] Without a depth of up-to-date knowledge, empathising becomes more difficult, which could leave a head coach with no idea what team members are thinking or feeling. An international rugby union head coach revealed how proactive he is in maintaining close relationships with his athletes: "I put things in place like coaches' cafés, where we get players to come and have a chat, one to one. If I haven't seen the players for a while, I'll schedule a five-minute meeting each just to talk about stuff other than rugby, more than five minutes if I can tell they need it. The more doses of these chats you have, the quicker you get to know your players."

Other head coaches have described to me the importance of taking advantage of opportunities whenever they arise, to discover more about an athlete and bring the relationship closer together. On journeys, for example, conversations can be had that have all kinds of benefits. A men's handball head coach told me, "When we go away to games, we have a lot of time on the bus to chat to them about anything. And you can strike up a conversation and share things in common and you feel more human to them. That gives them the chance to come to you more readily with sport-related, performance-related issues."

As an empathic leader, you must be careful about how you respond when team members approach. The way a head coach responds will impact the likelihood of the individual coming to speak to them in the future. Another head coach told me, "I can only imagine in those situations that if you don't feel comfortable talking to someone, you won't. Then the rest breaks down. It's hugely important they feel comfortable enough to come and speak." This puts the focus on issues of trust.

Trust

To be an empathic leader, your whole self must be empathic, rather than you just switching empathy on when engaged in specific leadership tasks. Your empathy will be working for you even when you're unaware of it. Studies have shown that the more empathic you are as a person, the more naturally you will acquire friends and social networks.[8] When a team member notices a leader's empathic approach to them, there is a realisation that their interests are being considered. This develops trust.[9] Trust is a major component of a high-quality relationship, and research has shown that leaders who develop high-quality relationships with their followers become successful leaders.[10] Studies have also shown that a leader's success tends to be based on the team member's perceptions of how trustworthy they are.[11, 12]

In relationships, trust works in tandem with empathy. It brings people together, and the closer they become, the more empathy develops. Trust also helps a leader to share responsibilities with others, aiding cohesion and alignment. As team members learn to trust their leader, they start contributing more, which leads to greater job satisfaction, wellbeing, and they feel a greater sense of safety and protection.[13]

When team members trust their leader, the leader becomes more popular too.[4] Popularity is important in leadership since it offers more influence. Greater influence will help to maintain a collective effort, in a set direction. Conversely, a lack of trust in a leader will limit the quality of relationships. Team members may become distant, which is not what the empathic leader wants. However, being too close can also prove problematic.

Distance

As an empathic leader becomes closer to team members, there is a risk of becoming too close.[14] Being too close can lead to bias, which will mean poor decision making due to over-empathising with particular individuals.[15, 16] A men's football head coach explained to me how his emotions have sometimes got the better of his thinking: "The emotional connections can affect your selection decisions – that has happened to me. I've thought, Jesus, I knew I shouldn't have started him, or I knew I should have, but you have to learn those lessons."

Sometimes a leader might decide that an emotional connection is worth factoring into the decision-making process. It might enhance trust, for example. An international football head coach told me that "potentially there are dangers of getting too close and having your vision clouded for decisions. I've probably, in the past, had a player around because I've felt strongly about him, I've liked him. When there's been another player with potentially more talent, but I didn't get the same emotional connection, I chose the first player. Was that right or wrong? Maybe the one I didn't have an emotional connection with feels the same, and that makes it more likely that I made the right decision. But then the other was a better player. It's not a regular problem but it's definitely happened." Working on these situations requires reflecting on emotional information, the relationships, and the context, and rationalising all the knowledge at hand.

When it comes to relationships, selection is always going to be a tough part of empathic leadership, as a women's ice hockey head coach explained: "I won the national championship four years ago. The toughest thing wasn't the games; it was the two players that didn't play. Everyone wants to play, and telling them was by far the toughest thing to do. Then last year I was assistant national coach in the Olympics and one of my former players, that I'd coached, was the last to be cut. She'd actually asked that I talk to her afterwards. She'd worked for four years towards that Olympics and so that is the toughest thing for a coach. If you don't feel bad about it, then you shouldn't be coaching. I don't think that anybody who coaches at those levels should do that easily. These players have put in as much time as the others."

Close emotional bonds with team members can make passing on bad news an incredibly difficult task. A women's international football head coach told me, "You don't like to be too close because often you have to give them bad news. The tricky bit is knowing that boundary." Knowing the personal circumstance of each team member can make things harder still. Empathy is about understanding needs on an individual level, but sometimes choices have to be made that put the team first. A rugby union head coach told me that "dropping players, especially when they are experienced players who are coming towards the end of their careers, can affect your relationships; it's definitely affected my relationships with some players who thought that right at the end they didn't get what they deserved. And I said to them that the only factor in any of these decisions is what's in the best interest of the team."

Empathising with disappointed team members is an important investment in leadership relationships, not only with the unlucky athlete; others will be aware of how you have managed the situation and acted towards them. Perceived empathy grows through narratives about the leader, as much as from personal experience. However, in certain situations, an empathic reputation can make a leader more vulnerable.

Empathic leaders must take care that they are not being taken advantage of once their empathic nature is recognised. As a leader, you need to remain vigilant about how genuine reported predicaments are. If you are perceived to be empathic, compassionate, and caring, team members may exaggerate their own distress.[17] Even with the advantages of the knowledge gained through close relationships, it can still be difficult to understand the intentions of less scrupulous individuals.[18] As the head coach of a men's ice hockey team told me, "You never really know with people. I had this one guy, who I thought I could trust, and I guess I didn't really know him as well as I thought." The more you know those you lead, the less open to exploitation you are likely to be. However, familiarity or becoming too close to a group can cause problems concerning the parameters of leadership.

There is a tendency for a leader to favour the familiar.[19] When a leader manages to maintain a balance across the group, in-group empathy will make the group stronger. However, the gap between the leader and other group members can become blurred. As a leader, you need to ensure that the gap still exists.

Maintaining an optimum distance isn't easy. A leader has decisions to make all of the time, often away from competition. A rugby union head coach told me, "I don't go out with the players; I'm double their age, but we won the league last Saturday and I did go out with them on the Sunday because all the coaches and staff went. But there came a point in the evening when I left, when I knew it was going to go somewhere else. It was important for them to see me there to celebrate, and I had some great conversations with people there throughout the evening. So I'm never going to go out on a Saturday night with the players – of course not – but it's important the players know you care. I think if you are too distant, it's a problem because the players think you *don't* care, and that you are only interested in how they've done rather than who they are. And that's a mistake, I think."

A head coach of a men's football team related a similar dilemma: "We went on a run a couple of years ago where we didn't lose for 13 games and got into a final; we won it, and then what happened was players became my best friends and it was party time! We were out a lot together, and as that period ended and we were setting ourselves up for the new season, a couple of the players were contacting me directly and asking me to go out for a drink and stuff like that. I had to really pull back from that and remind them that there is that line between the coach and the players and it's knowing when you overstep it. I have a network of close friends; I don't need the players as friends like that. I could also be seen out with certain players and then other players have an issue with it. Questions will be asked, and it has an effect on the whole environment."

Elite sport has found a way to manage this gap between the leader and the team. Leadership groups can act as a relational buffer between the head coach and team members. Whether members of these leadership groups are chosen by the head coaches themselves or by team members, the leadership group tends to include the more empathic team members, as an Australian head coach explained: "We have a playing leadership group, comprised of a couple of the senior players and a couple of younger players. I let the players decide who is in that group based on that. So then they have their own separate meeting. They look for players that they have respect for, but also who have respect for them, that if they have a question, they won't be judged for it, and they'll be supported. Overall, I think the one who is most empathic will always get chosen for that leadership group because they don't just want an idiot shouting at them."

A netball head coach mentioned empathy as soon as I asked her about a leadership group: "I've selected four senior players for that. It was the empathy that those four have for others in the group, that's why I chose them. The last of those four came late, and after three training sessions, I knew she was someone who understands other players and someone the others trusted and they'd go to her with things, straight away. One is more direct and another leads by example. I don't want the same type of people, you want the variety, each giving you something else, but you want them all to understand others."

The team captain also provides a buffer. The head coaches I've met have all said that they've taken empathic ability into their decisions of who to choose for the role. The head coach of a women's football team told me about his choice: "I thought that she was very caring, and group focused. Unselfish. For example, we had triallists in last week and obviously they'd travelled a long way; they are living in a house where they don't know any-body. They'd been in a day, and I called her in. I asked her what she was doing tomorrow night, she said nothing, and so I asked her to take the two triallists out for a meal and she said, 'Oh, we are doing that tonight.' I told her she was a legend and then she came back with feedback and that was great. I gave myself a pat on my back, I'd chosen the right person. I trust her a lot with regard to her feedback on other players. I've had players offered to me and I'll go to her if she knows them; she knows if they will sit within my values as a person. She understands me."

As leaders grow close to individuals or groups, outsiders are less easy to empathise with.[20] Although empathy is a positive thing for leadership, it can deepen divisions between groups. This may inhibit decisions to bring athletes into the first-team squad or impact relationships with athletes who arrive from rival clubs. The initial phase of these relationships will often be the most difficult. It may begin with a handshake, maybe even a hug. This might seem a small thing, but physical contact has a huge impact on relationships and suits a leader with empathic aspirations.[21]

Physical Contact in Relationships

Touch is part of human social bonding and facilitates resonance and behavioural synchrony.[22, 23] When we look at two human beings making skin-to-skin contact through a thermal imaging camera, we see heat. As the touch ends, the heat doesn't vanish. The effects last longer than the contact. Since empathic leadership is centred on closer relationships, physical contact is bound to become part of that relationship. When I've asked head coaches what images best describe empathic leadership in elite sport, the first they describe is a head coach embracing an athlete at the end of a game: the post-match hug.

A men's football head coach working in North America referred to one or two successful coaches he'd regularly see on television hugging their players at the end of matches: "You do see the younger generation, you could say, with a bit more touching and cuddling, hugs at the end of games." A football head coach from Scandinavia pointed out that "some also hug players from the opposition team!" This is further evidence of the personality of empathic leaders running consistently through their interactions with other people. As an international hockey head coach told me, "Hugs might be given after someone does something well. Other times, it's an arm around the shoulder because things haven't gone well. It definitely shows empathy." Once again, it is worth remembering that the display of empathy is not only taken in by the individual athlete, but all those observing the behaviour.

Going around hugging people at random would be socially unacceptable and ineffective leadership. This is particularly true if such behaviour is out of character. Authenticity, like empathy, begins with an understanding of one's self. An international lacrosse head coach explained: "A non-tactile coach being overly physical with no warning could make the players very uncomfortable."

The context and relationship in each situation must be understood, and an empathic leader will be skilled in maintaining such understanding. An English head coach explained that when engaging in physical contact with team members, "it cannot come from a textbook, it has to come from within". Hugging must be part of who the head coach is and who the athlete is, and knowing the athlete well is key. An international hockey head coach described a slightly different but no less empathic approach: "Some will come for a hug. I never try to hug *them*. It has to be them leaning to me. It has to be authentic, not falsified. Sometimes coaches do it to give the appearance of a happy family, but you can see the player's reaction isn't as authentic as it should be."

The end of the game represents a major hugging moment in sport today. Again, this must be tailored for each individual context. A football head coach told me, "There are players that I'd hug. There are times and moments when it depends on the person and the moment. We lost two-one last weekend in the 93rd minute, from an offside goal, and my players had given everything, and they were in tears, like they'd lost a cup final. I've known some of these players for a few years and I know their families, and there is a young player crying in front of me. It's natural. I'm a father, you know. I do feel like a bit of a dad to some of these players and you just give them a hug. It just has to be natural."

It's clear that hugging symbolises a new way of leading in elite sport. The head coach of a men's football team explained, "Hugging highlights different styles of management now. It's the younger generation, you could say, with a bit more touching and cuddling, hugs at the end of games. It shows how coaching is different now."

Another football head coach, in his late 50s, told me that he is not a hugger, "No, I am a dinosaur! I am too late to change to be like this. These people you mention, they are ten years younger than me; for me, it's not me. I envy them in a way, but it's not me. You can't go around hugging people if they don't put their arms up to be hugged. They wouldn't expect it from me, it's not natural to me. Never did a coach hug me when I played. I won't do it." Some months later, this head coach emailed me with photographs of him hugging two of his players at the end of a game. "As you can see from the pictures, I turned hugger!" he said.

For all head coaches, the timing and feeling must be right. By knowing themselves and each individual team member as a person, awkward situations can be avoided. An international football head coach explained how he modifies his behaviour to suit an individual: "Some are not comfortable with a hug, so it can be a hand slap." This maintains the relationship going forward rather than making either person feel uncomfortable. Similarly, reacting to individual performances can influence future relationships and the confidence of an athlete. An international lacrosse head coach explained to me how he shows that one performance won't threaten a relationship: "You know, he's not playing as well as he normally does. Do I blame him? Do I get on his back? Do I bitch and moan? No, you know. I love him unequivocally." This approach reassures the athlete, who, through one moment of physical contact, understands that no matter what happens, their relationship is safe. But there may be situations where a hug makes a team member feel *less* safe.

It has become more common in recent years for there to be gender differences between a team and a head coach. Gender can influence how team members want to be treated,[24] and care needs to be taken about physical intimacy.[21] A female head coach of a women's football team told me, "I think it's harder for men if they are coaching women." A female head coach of a men's team told me that "a male, coaching female athletes, should not take the initiative when it comes to hugging".

Gender and Cultural Differences

Women are generally underrepresented in sport leadership positions.[25, 26] This increases the likelihood of male head coaches leading female teams. In the past, when male head coaches have led teams of female athletes, they've tended to reproduce ideas about gender that dominated during their playing years, rather than updating their understanding.[27] An empathic approach will be less influenced by outdated ideas and more interested in keeping knowledge up to date with dynamic communication and close relationships with team members.

Research shows that women score higher than men on self-reported empathy scales.[28] However, this may be due to gender-biased societal expectations. Empathic displays have been shown to be different too. Women tend to employ the facial gestures and vocabulary that we associate with empathy more than men.[29] This is consistent with the idea of *stereotype lift*, where group identity reminds individuals to up their performance in certain observed behaviours.[30, 31]

Shared experiences can influence empathy too, and so men are likely to find it easier to empathise with other men, and women with other women. If any of this is true, male head coaches of female teams begin with a disadvantage.

Understanding gender perspectives should be part of empathic leadership and is unlikely to have been a leadership focus two decades ago, as this male head coach of a women's team explained: "Whereas a coach 20 years ago wouldn't change their style, now you have to understand that managing women's football is very different." A male head coach of a women's ice hockey team considered how he altered his practices when he began to lead teams of women: "There's obviously a few things different about coaching women. I might go out for a drink with a group of men, but I wouldn't go out with a group of women, or one or two women – it just looks wrong. Someone might get the wrong idea or start a rumour, and it's just not worth the risk." He also noted the differences in relationships between team members: "Guys are much more direct with each other. They don't have that concern; there's no hard feelings or grudges. Girls are different; they are direct on each other, but a girl can stay mad for a while. I had to understand that women have a different team culture to men."

Another male head coach of a women's team told me that "female athletes have tighter bonds. I'd say they are more empathic. They understand each other better. The men can become a team for the game, then hate each other when they come off the court, and it doesn't seem to matter. Ideally, I want them all to get on, of course."

The gender differences between a head coach and the team add further complications to physical touch and hugging. A female head coach of a women's team acknowledged that "it's harder for men if they are coaching women". A male head coach of a women's team said he often found it difficult: "I'd be more careful with women, younger ones in particular." Another male head coach of a women's team offered a more detailed explanation of the way he approaches his work: "I'm quite a big man and might be seen as intimidating. I mean, you know me, I'm not like that, but just from my size, I'm aware. I think that understanding of the person is the major thing, and I've always erred massively on the side of caution. I worked in the female under-16 game for a long time, and I was always protecting myself, as well as anything else it's important. This day and age, we make sure that in any meetings we have there's another female member of staff present. We have a female physio – she's massively important to us, a huge link. I think if we didn't have a female staff member, it would be a huge issue for us. So I'd always encourage that. I wouldn't want me to be the only male; I think a mixture is important."

A female head coach of a men's team told me that she believes that her unique situation offers certain advantages: "Before our team plays, they all hug me individually. It might sound weird, and it's not happened to me so much with women. Because the men are being coached by a woman, it reduces the testosterone, and they kind of view me as a mum and they are more respectful. They are an aggressive team. I'd hate to see what they'd be like if they were led by an aggressive male. They'd go too far. I can bring them back down quickly."

Whether it is down to gender, background, or something else, an empathic leader will focus on the team culture of the group they lead, learning all the behaviours, rules, and intricacies of that world. In the modern era, a sports team can be made up of athletes with a variety of backgrounds, which provides its own challenge. It's not just athletes who move between countries and cultures; Head Coaches do too.

Understanding someone from a different culture from one's own requires deeper efforts to comprehend that person's unique cultural circumstances. Gender and cultural differences may inhibit the use of leader empathy until a passage of time allows a head coach to gain understanding through growing relationships with team members.

Most of the head coaches I've spoken to have worked in Europe, Australasia, and North America, but two conveyed their experiences of working in China and an entirely different cultural environment. One of these head coaches told me that "it would have taken a long time to get on the same page, and we didn't get that time". His tenure was ended. He told me that this was because those above him didn't like to see his athletes enjoying training as much as they seemed to be. The other head coach had a similar story: "It is possible that Chinese culture is behind the curve, when it comes to empathic leadership in sport, or that it will never be ready for it." It's possible that a more empathic approach will never be possible in an authoritarian culture. However, if empathic leadership works as well in China as it has in other parts of the world, the teams and organisations that persevere with it will gain a significant advantage over those who refuse.

It is said that empathy has the potential to transcend demographic barriers.[4] Whatever their gender, cultural differences, or background, empathic head coaches have the ability to build relationships and promote wellbeing across diverse groups. Appointing head coaches according to their gender or cultural backgrounds is unnecessary. An empathic leader has the tools to understand such differences and create bonds regardless.

A Multitude of Relationships

In elite sport today, head coaches have many more people to understand and build relationships with than did their predecessors. The head coach of a women's football team explained that "there are staff within head office, finance, logistics, media, marketing, promotions. I have to have relationships with all of these people. Sponsors, commercial partners, parents, family, friends of athletes. You try to have a relationship with all of these, and all have different objectives and want different outcomes. Trying to understand them and be empathic is always beneficial." Given that empathy brings people closer together, it is helpful in all working relationships. However, maintaining these additional relationships creates extra stress.

A head coach working in Australia at international level told me that "there are far more moving parts to it now, the events day people, media, marketing people, the ones above you. As coaches, we underestimate the number of people we come into contact with and need to understand. You need to manage all of these people, in some respect, in order to do your job successfully. We go into the game thinking it's about managing players, but it doesn't end there. The reality is it's about a lot of things, and if you don't manage each group of people well, any one of them can give you just as much of a problem as the players. Add supporters to that too!"

Researchers have recognised the importance of empathy in relationships with customers across industries including elite sport.[32–35] Fans are considered powerful stakeholder customers, more so than customers in other industries.[25] Head coaches have a responsibility to understand fan perspectives. An international head coach said, "This is elite sport, it's entertainment. Without people to entertain, we have no industry. So we must consider their perspective. The sports that succeed have a quality experience for the fans and so we need to understand what they want." Empathy is key to this understanding. Having an empathic relationship with the fans has become an accepted responsibility of head coaches in elite sport today, who are aware of the consequences of ignoring it. A men's football head coach explained that "there's a need to have a relationship with the fans, there's a need to understand their perspective. You need to understand they're entitled to have an opinion and their own view. You don't necessarily agree with their view, but you give the fans what they need. That's a massive relationship because that's a relationship that keeps you in a job or gets you the sack."

As an international football head coach told me, "small things for the fans mean a lot. I try to imagine how they see me and what I do. It has to be as truthful as it can be, but some things can't be shared. It has to be respectful and at the end of the day you have to appreciate what their realities are. I'm lucky enough to do what I do. I'm not digging a ditch, and there are some very good people digging ditches, but it's not the greatest job in the world, so they live vicariously through their team or national team." What is important to fans varies from one club to another, and by sport.

A cricket head coach explained what he understands is important to his club's fans: "If we put out 11 home-grown players and lost every game, they wouldn't give a shit. When I'm communicating with the wider public, I try to explain what our long-term goal is. We are trying to create a team with ten home-grown players and a world-class overseas. We're not far away. We have eight in there. Then the fans see it's authentic. That bigger picture is vital, and it buys you time. If we are doing badly results-wise, people are more patient and empathic."

Patience and empathy tend to run both ways in healthy relationships,[36] but it can be frustrating for leaders when their customers, or fans, are unaware of the reality of the team's situation. The head coach of a women's football team explained that "supporters are more aware and have a better understanding, but not of implementing things, and they don't have patience. If you are trying to implement a certain playing style, you need 60 training sessions. They don't understand that."

The growing awareness of fans has been fuelled by media technology, and this can help with transparency. It should lead to fans having more empathy for the head coach and team. A head coach of a men's football team described his own situation: "We have a really good engagement with social media platforms, and they have a good connection with the club. The fans get a good insight with the day-to-day stuff going on, and I think that brings a good understanding both ways."

Of all the different relationships the head coaches mentioned, it was the relationships with those above them that were reported to pose the greatest problems. In many cases, this was put down to a lack of empathy towards them. One head coach told me, "So far, I've found the sporting director is very emotionally led, which worries me, to be honest. One day I came in and he was patting my back, just because someone told him training was going well, and he's in seventh heaven. A week later, I saw him, and he didn't even look up at me, so that's what can happen, and it's worrying."

Likewise, another head coach described his frustrations with the hier-archy: "The people above me, the governing body, etc. They can be an issue. They are not always people who have played or coached at all, or some-times people who have played or coached other sports and that limits their understanding of my situation. How can they empathise well if they've never been in a situation anything like the one I'm in? In other countries, where the sport is bigger, it's more often people from our sport, which is favourable." The priorities of those above the head coach should be clearly focused on the team's performance; however, in some situations described to me, individuals have prioritised themselves.

One international head coach believes that those above can often be jealous of the close relationships between the head coach and athletes. He told me that "the NGB (national governing body) saw my close relationship with the players as an erosion of power and control. They want to control the sport. As a coach, I had a fantastic relationship with the players, and they saw that as a threat. They've done a good job of bringing in people from outside who give a veneer of credibility to process and systems, but they've never seen a training session, met a player or me. Externally, it looks great, but to us at the operational sharp end, it's a nonsense; we never see them, we don't have a relationship with them at all. Maybe it's forgivable, but the talent manager, who in theory oversees my working world, came to one training session and that was to talk about a kit deal. She never came to watch and observe, be a critical friend, ask, 'Why are you doing this or that?' What made it worse from the players' perspective was the managers coming on all the tours. So while you're flogging your guts out, they're nowhere to be seen. When you're at an event with a bit of profile, you know, more glitz or glamour or sunshine, they're all over it. Our talent manager will almost invariably bolt a holiday on with family members. I try to view things through other people's eyes, but I thought, 'Why would she do that, what are the reasons for that approach?' From the players' perspective, it's just a piss-take. The real difficulty that I have is that it leads to an issue for the talent manager because she sees the players don't have a relationship with her and then she asks me why. Then it looks like it's a failure of my culture – they don't see that it's their behaviour. There's no alignment of culture outside of the player group; if there's one failure that I made, it's not being effective at managing upwards."

In all of the relationships described, an empathic leader will be aware of being observed. What others see, particularly team members, will have an impact on performance, relationships, and the tenure of the head coach. It was interesting to hear what can change when a head coach takes a different attitude to a relationship. In the following example, that relationship was with a rival head coach: "I had a temperamental relationship with a coach from another team and we had and still have a great rivalry. We have a young squad. We always hit each other at loggerheads, if you like, but I think we've got to know each other better and I've tried to make our engagements more pleasurable, and I've got that back from them and we've seen the teams have more respect for each other as a result. We had a surprise victory against them in the cup this year, and they were very gracious in defeat, and I'd never seen that from them before. I think if your players see that animosity there between coaches, they will act in the same way. Then they are not focusing on what you want them to do technically or tactically."

For empathic leaders, all relationships are important, but priority has to be the relationships with team members. In elite sport, these tend to be closer than ever before and they enhance trust and an alignment of ideas. Whatever the gender, culture, or background of team members, empathic leaders will skilfully create bonds close enough to be physical when appropriate, and this physicality brings people closer still. With a multitude of relationships requiring careful management, and empathic leaders being skilled at "reading people", it is no wonder that sports organisations are increasingly focusing on empathy as a desirable leadership quality.

Notes

1. Marques, J. (2015). The changed leadership landscape: What matters today. *Journal of Management Development*, 34(10), 1310–1322.
2. Kingsley Westerman, C. Y., Reno, K. M. & Heuett, K. B. (2018). Delivering feedback: Supervisors' source credibility and communication competence. *International Journal of Business Communication*, 55(4), 526–546.
3. Stajkovic, A. D. & Luthans, F. (1998). Self-efficacy and work-related performance: A meta-analysis. *Psychological Bulletin*, 124(2), 240–261.
4. Tzouramani, E. (2017). Leadership and empathy. In J. Marques & S. Dhiman (Eds), *Leadership today: Practices for personal and professional development* (pp. 197–216). Springer. doi:10.1007/978-3-319-31036-7_11
5. Humphrey, R. H. (2002). The many faces of emotional leadership. *Leadership Quarterly*, 13(5), 493–504.
6. Orben, A., Tomova, L. & Blakemore, S. J. (2020). The effects of social deprivation on adolescent development and mental health. *Lancet Child and Adolescent Health*, 4(8), 634–640.
7. Carroll, P., Roth, Y. & Garin, K. A. (2011). *Win forever: Live, work, and play like a champion*. Portfolio/Penguin.
8. Kardos, P., Leidner, B., Pléh, C., Soltész, P. & Unoka, Z. (2017). Empathic people have more friends: Empathic abilities predict social network size and position in social network predicts empathic efforts. *Social Networks*, 50, 1–5.
9. Morelli, S. A., Ong, D. C., Makati, R., Jackson, M. O. & Zaki, J. (2017). Empathy and well-being correlate with centrality in different social networks. *Proceedings of the National Academy of Sciences of the United States of America*, 114(37), 9843–9847.
10. Mahsud, R., Yukl, G. & Prussia, G. (2010). Leader empathy, ethical leadership, and relations-oriented behaviors as antecedents of leader-member exchange quality. *Journal of Management Psychology*, 25(6), 561–577.

11. Lester, S. W. & Brower, H. H. (2003). In the eyes of the beholder: The relationship between subordinates' felt trustworthiness and their work attitudes and behaviors. *Journal of Leadership and Organizational Studies, 10*(2), 17–33.

12. Zampetakis, L. A. & Moustakis, V. (2011). Managers' trait emotional intelligence and group outcomes: The case of group job satisfaction. *Small Group Research, 42*(1), 77–102.

13. Kohlrieser, G., Goldsworthy, S. & Coombe, D. (2012). *Care to dare: Unleashing astonishing potential through secure base leadership.* Jossey-Bass.

14. Solomon, G. & Lobinger, B. (2011). Sources of expectancy information among coaches: A cross cultural investigation. *Theories and Applications, 1*(1), 46–57.

15. Drewe, S. (2002). The coach–athlete relationship: How close is too close? *Journa of the Philosophy of Sport, 29*(2), 174–181.

16. Lorimer, R. (2013). The development of empathic accuracy in sports coaches. *Journal of Sport Psychology in Action, 4*(1), 26–33.

17. Kleinlogel, E. & Dietz, J. (2013). Ethical decision making in organizations. In K. Pavlovich & K. Krahnke (Eds), *Organizing through empathy* (pp. 116–129). Routledge.

18. Adams, R. B. *et al.* (2010). Cross-cultural reading the mind in the eyes: An fMRI investigation. *Journal of Cognitive Neuroscience, 22*(1), 97–108.

19. Vanman, E. J. (2016). The role of empathy in intergroup relations. *Current Opinion in Psychology, 11*, 59–63.

20. Kwon, D. (2017). The limits of empathy. *Psychologist, 30*, 28–32.

21. Munro, D., Powis, D. & Bore, M. (2013). Predicting empathy in medical students and doctors. In K. Pavlovich & K. Krahnke (Eds), *Organizing through empathy* (pp. 147–165). Routledge.

22. Chatel-Goldman, J., Congedo, M., Jutten, C. & Schwartz, J.-L. (2014). Touch increases autonomic coupling between romantic partners. *Frontiers in Behavioral Neuroscience, 8*, 95.

23. Goldstein, P., Weissman-Fogel, I. & Shamay-Tsoory, S. (2017). The role of touch in regulating inter-partner physiological coupling during empathy for pain. *Scientific Reports, 7*, 3252.

24. Boatwright, K. J. & Forrest, L. (2000). Leadership preferences: The influence of gender and needs for connection on workers' ideal preferences for leadership behaviors. *Journal of Leadership Studies, 7*(2), 18–34.

25. Peachey, J. W., Zhou, Y., Damon, Z. J. & Burton, L. J. (2015). Forty years of leadership research in sport management: A review, synthesis, and conceptual framework. *Journal of Sport Management, 29*(5), 570–587.

26. Burton, L. J., Kane, G. M. & Borland, J. F. (2020). *Sport leadership in the 21st century.* Jones & Bartlett Learning.

27. De Haan, D. & Knoppers, A. (2019). Gendered discourses in coaching high-performance sport. *International Review for the Sociology of Sport, 55*(6), 1–16. doi:10.1177/1012690219829692

28. Davis, M. H. (1983). Measuring individual differences in empathy: Evidence for a multidimensional approach. *Journal of Personality and Social Psychology, 44*(1), 113–126.

29. Breithaupt, F. & Hamilton, A. B. B. (2019). *The dark sides of empathy.* Cornell University Press.

30. Walton, G. M. & Cohen, G. L. Stereotype lift. (2003). *Journal of Experimental Social Psychology, 39*(5), 456–467.

31. Marx, D. M. & Stapel, D. A. (2006). Understanding stereotype lift: On the role of the social self. *Social Cognition, 24*(6), 776–792.

32. Costa, G. & Glinia, E. (2003). Empathy and sport tourism services: A literature review. *Journal of Sport and Tourism, 8*(4), 284–292.

33. Peppard, J. (2000). Customer relationship management (CRM) in financial services. *European Management Journal, 18*(3), 312–327.

34. Pavlovich, K. & Krahnke, K. (Eds) (2013). *Organizing through empathy.* Routledge.

35. Amato, C., Bodkin, C. D. & Peters, C. (2010). Building a fan community through the folklore of NASCAR. *International Journal of Sport Management and Marketing, 8*(1/2), 5–20.

36. Bazalgette, P. (2017). *The empathy instinct: How to create a more civil society.* John Murray.

Empathic Climates   **4**

Like many industries, elite sport has provided too many examples of toxic climates or climates of fear, in which people have suffered and potential is wasted.[1] The worst of these reports include allegations of bullying, physical or sexual abuse, and chronic mental health conditions arising as a result of time spent within a specific organisation or team environment. Sadly, several of these reports have centred on sports academies where children have suffered at the hands of abusive coaches, and where other leaders have turned a blind eye. Such climates are often said to lack empathy. An empathic climate is a safe climate, with safety promoted by empathic leadership and empathy between team members.

From youth to full professional level, human beings have suffered at the hands of leaders who lack empathy. Things may not always be as bad as the worst examples mentioned, but where the climate is one of fear, the leadership tends to be direct and to lean towards bullying.[2] These conditions fuel toxicity and fear.[3] Team members become victims; their wellbeing suffers and so does their performance. Studies have also shown that a lack of leader empathy leads to disengagement.[4] Climates of fear are considered immoral and ineffective, yet in many cases they manage to prevail for longer than you would think.

A climate of fear is self-protecting, with those within it fearing retribution or loss of position for speaking out.[5] A leader who has spent years of effort climbing to the top might be unwilling to risk everything by speaking out against a toxic leadership or culture, even when it involves the worst kinds of abuse. The stakes become higher as the competition becomes more serious. This may explain why climates of fear have been discovered at international level, including paralympic teams,[6] in elite sport all over

DOI: 10.4324/9781003324676-5

the world.[7, 8] Although short-term success is always possible, such climates are unsustainable and eventually lead to underperformance as athletes are drained by stress and grow more cynical and distrustful of leaders.[9]

Whether directly or indirectly, fear and toxicity stem from the leadership and soon spread throughout a group, negatively impacting relationships within it. In such a climate, team members treat each other with suspicion rather than trust and camaraderie. Leadership goals, like cohesion, become impossible to achieve. A climate of safety has far more to offer individuals, teams, and organisations.[10]

Psychological Safety

Psychological safety refers to being in a context without experiencing fear of negative consequences to self-image, status, or career.[11] A psychologically safe climate will stimulate feelings of emotional safety, respect, and trust when interacting with another person,[12] meaning risk taking is less daunting.[11]

The importance of psychological safety is now becoming widely accepted, yet it appears to have been expressed by the American psychologist Carl Rogers over half a century ago.[13] Rogers prescribed what he called *an atmosphere* of safety. In Roger's prescribed world, listening and understanding promote safety, and there is freedom of expression, rather than feelings of fear, threat, and judgement. This focuses on climate rather than culture. The atmosphere, or climate, is vulnerable to change, dependent on current leadership styles and policies, whereas organisational culture is often held in place by tradition and is relatively stable over time.[14]

Organisational culture is defined by the assumptions and values that guide life within an organisation. In elite sport, culture is often referred to in terms of a team, but the whole organisation will have its own culture that will interact and influence that of the team. A leader's relationships across an organisation can be influential; as we know, emotions and empathy are contagious. Leaders need to create a culture that motivates and attracts talent if they desire success.[15] By maintaining a safe team climate, a leader will make progress in improving team culture.

Empathic leaders understand the value of safe climates, team culture, and the sense of community, and they know that they are responsible for their creation. Head coaches working in elite sport today have described to me climates of fear that they endured when they were athletes. An international football head coach told me that the whole climate in his playing days was, "based on fear of the gaffer." Another football head coach told me, "Climate wasn't really mentioned in those days, atmosphere maybe, but there wasn't much focus on it, as far as I could tell."

Thankfully, times have changed. The head coach of a rugby union team summed up what all of the head coaches I have met have told me – that "safety is a huge thing for us" – and an ice hockey head coach confirmed that, "Safety has become a target for elite coaches."

However, striving for safety is more complicated than you might think. Team members need to be motivated, each in a unique way. Although a leader can tailor their behaviour towards each athlete, the climate has to serve the whole group. As an international hockey head coach told me, perspectives can contradict what is going on. He said, "I think a safe climate is really important, but you might get one saying there's bullying and another saying that he drove us to a gold medal." Getting this right requires regular and empathic communication and growing close relationships, full of honesty and trust.

If leaders lack empathy, it will negatively influence the climate.[16] The interrelated experiences people have at work depend on the state of the climate. This may refer to large organisations or smaller groups like teams, and not only in sport. Empathy is particularly important as a leadership skill today due to the increasing use of teams across industries, which is another reason why empathic leaders are now valued so highly.

The Role of Empathic Leaders

Empathic leaders have the tools to manage team and organisational climates towards safety. Head coaches in elite sport today have come to understand the consequences of fear and toxicity, and are determined to pursue climate safety, where team members are more likely to fulfil their potential. In a safe climate, everyone can maintain their own wellbeing and enjoy coming to work.

A football head coach told me that she was aware of reports of "'toxic climates' or 'climates of fear' if you like; in other sports, including some at national level, and we definitely want to stay away from that. I want my players to look forward to coming to training, and I know that human beings flourish in climate safety."

Climate safety is high on the list of the leadership aims of the head coaches I have met. Once again, it seems part of who these leaders are as people, as much as it is about their leadership strategy. For an international lacrosse head coach, it is right at the top of his list of leadership goals: "I could lose one hundred games and probably, if it was in the right environment,

I could probably sleep at night, but if I ever thought there was a hint of toxic behaviour, or what I believe to be toxic behaviour, in my group, I would feel like I'd failed. So, yes, a key driver for us is to ensure that that environment would never be allowed to flourish."

It is not just the head coach who influences the team climate, but as leaders they are responsible for climates and so the behaviour and communications of team members have to be managed. The head coach of a cricket team offered some good examples: "I can think of one instance, playing against a strong opposition, the young lad was bowling and he was getting smacked, and they nicknamed him 'Boards', because they kept hitting the ball to the boards. Now you think, that's funny; however, he is carrying that emotional baggage now. You don't know what damage it's doing. You see when someone throws in to the wicket keeper, it's not great and the keeper gives him some stick, the next one they throw, they're tentative. If they make a mistake, we'll practise throwing and do some work on it; I want the honesty, but not the piss-taking sense. Although it still happens. I'm constantly on at the guys about the way they communicate because you've got no idea what's going on inside someone else's head. I could take the piss and it be funny, but a young guy could go home and say to himself, 'Fucking hell, did the head coach mean that?' That makes his job harder."

A harsh team climate increases the stress on the athlete, whereas a feeling of safety will have a positive influence on their wellbeing and performance.[17] A rugby union head coach told me that, in his environment, "the team is encouraged to respect the individuality of other members, allowing athletes to feel safe enough to be themselves". He explained to me that he reiterates to his players how important their words can be. He said, "One of the things we constantly talk to the team about is tolerance – well, tolerance is a terrible word, you shouldn't feel like you have to tolerate someone. But what we talk about is that everybody brings something different to the table and we demand that those differences are respected, that we focus on what people bring, not what they can't bring, what they can do, not what they can't do, and it's kind of all those ingredients combined which make the squad and the group operate healthily. It's easy to say, but difficult to put into practice over a ten-year period, but that tolerance, for want of a better word, of each individual and allowing them to be themselves, is critical."

This atmosphere or climate created by empathic leadership not only helps with wellbeing and performance, but allows athletes to feel safe enough to make a contribution to the development of the team. This is important in creating a more innovative and creative environment that will also improve performance.[18] The head coach of a women's international team described the efforts and resources that are invested in his team environment to ensure team members feel safe. He told me that a six-year psychology programme hadn't delivered, "but now we have the right person in charge and he's performance focused. If you get it wrong, you don't get creativity because people aren't prepared to speak out."

Research has confirmed that a lack of safety can harm performance by inhibiting creativity.[19, 20] Safety allows team members to behave in a more open and honest manner.[21] Rather than dominating decision making, empathic leaders encourage team members to contribute, and to feel free to be honest rather than feeling threatened when consulted. When team members feel threatened, their contribution to the organisation is inhibited, and subsequently this restricts innovation.[22]

Organisations across industries are constantly looking for ways to nurture innovation.[23] This is for good reason as studies have shown how much innovation improves performance.[24] Safety, wellbeing, and job satisfaction all play a role in this.[18, 25] In a team with high psychological safety, members feel confident that no one will embarrass or punish anyone else for admitting a mistake, asking a question, or offering a new idea.

Valuing the expression of honest opinions encourages people to speak up, and this is as contagious as empathy itself. The head coach of a cricket team told me, "I'm a big believer in learning when we win. If we lose, okay, let's park it and come back to it when we do an analysis. So I went quite hard on them after a win. One of the senior players said, 'You know what, I fucked up today.' It was so powerful because it's a guy everyone respects. We had a new coach operating with us; he's worked in international cricket, and one of the biggest counties in England, three other counties – you know, vastly experienced. He said, 'I've never seen that. That's unbelievably powerful.' And to me it's started to become the norm. It's really exciting that people are comfortable to do that because we make mistakes, you're going to. If you are the best in the world, 50 per cent of the time you're not performing. So you make mistakes. I'll always talk honestly, and I value that in others."

When an example is set by an empathic leader or a team member is well received, it will be followed by other members of the group. The resultant behaviours are altruistic, and the environment becomes more caring.[26]

Research has shown that when youth footballers perceive a caring environment, they become more likely to express caring behaviours towards their teammates.[27] Caring behaviour enhances the safety of the climate and makes toxic events (such as bullying and anti-social behaviour) less likely.[28] Caring sports teams develop a set of normal behaviours, rituals, and values based on the idea of understanding and caring for others. This can be supported by specific caring practices such as the promotion of inclusion, acceptance, and group decision making.[29]

Empathic leaders instil a caring culture through their behaviours. Rather than forcing team members to take part, the leader might wait for them to notice the value of an action, and then participate voluntarily themselves.[30] As behaviours and rituals become familiar, a shared history takes shape, emotional connections grow, and this becomes the culture. Used to a safe and caring climate, and feeling part of the team culture, a group will become closer still and everyone will enjoy a sense of community.[31]

Once a sense of community exists, it becomes easier to create the solidarity, team cohesion, and harmony needed to pursue shared goals. Empathy brings people together by recognising how we as humans can connect with and depend on each other. This is very different from merely being a collection of individuals.

The quality and closeness of relationships between a leader and team members will enhance athlete commitment levels. However, the quality of the whole environment and the sense of community may lead to expressed commitment from other staff who work around the team. This occurred at a rugby union club whose head coach told me, "One of the joys for me is we've got an elite team, and a second team of younger players. On a Monday, the younger players played away, and there's a bit of travel involved, and we have physios and other staff who don't need to watch those games, but they'll go anyway. They go because they care about their players and want to see how they do. For me, it's unreal that that can happen. We want people to really care about the club that they work for, care about the group, and have it in their skin a little bit, you know." I asked this head coach if that level of commitment had always been there. He said, "No, ten years ago, that didn't exist at all. We've changed the environment and it does now."

Empathic leaders spread empathy throughout the teams and organisations they work in.[9, 32] Empathy is *caught* from a leader and soon transfers to other individuals, and before you know it, the whole environment is infected.[33–35] A head coach of a men's football team recognised that an environment where everyone feels safe and cared for "creates conditions for improved athletic performance. These are athletes working in competitive worlds. Anything that gives them an edge is useful. Why would I want them working in conditions that held them back?"

In order to manage a safe climate, empathic leaders remain aware of their responsibility to understand environments, which in sport are open to regular change and so require change management.[36] The head coach of an international women's team explained, "As any sport changes, the manager has to feel that change and deal with the new problems it brings. Now in the women's game, whereas they were once happy to get paid, now they are negotiating contracts and saying, 'Hey, she's getting this, so I want that.'

So, as the women's game is getting more professional, perhaps the team dynamic will edge towards the individual thought process like the men."

Empathic leaders adjust to new situations fast, and they engage in close relationships with similar pace. This is especially relevant in elite sport where turnover of athletes and head coaches can be fast.[37] Sport leaders are expected to adapt fast, and demonstrate and maintain positive emotions.[38]

Empathy helps to quickly create and then maintain safe climates in the elite sport team environment by acting as a connecting force, not only between the head coach and team members, but also between teammates.[39] Empathy also helps leaders to recognise links between emotions and behaviours.[40] Then it is just a matter of managing these emotions.

Managing Emotions

Since the turn of the century, organisational researchers have been focusing on managing emotions in the working environment.[41] The emotional aspects of the workplace influence the achievements of teams and organisations,[42] and so it would seem foolish for leaders to ignore emotions in the workplace.[43] Emotional management begins with empathy.[44]

Emotions help us survive, thrive, and avoid danger. They inspire our decisions, allow other people to understand us, and allow us to understand others. Leaders in elite sport recognise the importance of managing emotions and have changed their leadership practices and developed the appropriate skills to achieve this. The management of emotions is considered to be an integral skill of the empathic leader.[45]

Empathic leaders are adept at perceiving emotional undercurrents and managing them positively – for example, perceiving conflict as an opportunity for progression.[46] Empathy allows leaders to understand and successfully manage conflict in relationships, employing the right approach for each situation.[32] Managing emotions positively requires leaders to build close relationships with their team members in order to understand how to help them to progress. When leaders in elite sport talk about this work, they often refer to an emotional climate.

The emotional climate is the predominant collective emotions shared by members of social groups in a particular setting.[47] The emotional climate of a whole organisation is defined by how a member of an organisation perceives the feelings of the majority of its members in the situation constructed by the organisation.[48] The emotional climate of a team can be different from that of an organisation as a whole, and emotions can change and spread with haste within or between the two.

Both positive and negative emotions are contagious; however, an empathic leader can use this to create supportive atmospheres.[49] Psychologists have described emotional contagion as primitive empathy, since it often acts as a precursor to an empathic experience.[50] Emotional contagion is literally the catching of someone else's mood. Sometimes this involves catching an emotion while being unaware of it being caught and it turning up as your own feeling. This is referred to in Chapter 1 on self-empathy.[51] For example, a room full of babies becomes a very loud place shortly after one starts to cry.[52] By knowing others better, a leader seems more likely to avoid such misconceptions. Emotional sensitivity is thought to be positively correlated with higher-quality relationships.[53] Research has shown that leaders who successfully manage emotions induce improvements in performance, largely due to the positive influence on psychological wellbeing.[54]

Empathy allows leaders to recognise and understand the emotions across a team and helps them to understand when and where to draw points of view from across a group to ensure emotions are balanced.[55] Empathic leaders not only understand current emotional environments but also the possibilities bubbling away within. This ability also allows a leader to include everyone and to spot potential issues before they escalate.[56]

An empathic leader is a resonant leader, deciphering the emotions of a team by understanding their own feelings as well as those of the group. In elite sport, this enables head coaches to notice inner-state changes before directing athletes positively.[45] Empathic leaders are hyper-aware, constantly scanning their environment and adding knowledge to their database. It is this deepening of understanding that continues to inform future decisions and communications which will fuel a climate of safety.

Empathy establishes an unspoken mental and emotional connection, which reveals the hidden meanings behind words and body language.[57] The advantages are clear: by accepting and exploring the hidden undercurrents that affect human behaviour, it is possible to gain a better understanding of people, teams, organisations, and all of their complexities.[58]

There are certain situations common to elite sport where managing emotions becomes paramount. The emotions felt immediately after competition may be particularly volatile. The head coaches that I have spoken to all stated the importance of reflecting before reacting. This limits any potentially negative impact that may be inflicted upon the team climate. By understanding that athletes may display negative reactions, a head coach is demonstrating empathy. Reacting to this negativity would be a risk. A conversation immediately after a disappointing result is often best avoided. The head coach of a women's football team told me, "We have a rule, we play on Sundays; Mondays we don't see each other. I tell players that I don't want to hear from them after the game on the Sunday or all day Monday. If it's something really important, then, of course, no problems at all. But if it's something about the game, come to me on Tuesday and we can talk about it. It gives them reflection time . . . You know what it's like immediately after a game, but by Tuesday they have probably spoken to someone else, got another perspective, calmed down, and it gives us the opportunity to talk face to face."

Another example of a challenging time to manage emotions when leading teams in elite sport is when the game is in progress. The head coach is banished to the sidelines, but leadership is still required. Whether it's through a break in play or when an athlete drifts towards the sideline, team members always find time to look across to their leader during competition. In such situations, empathic leaders keep in mind that emotions are contagious.[19, 20] It is important to understand that a head coach's touchline behaviour offers both risk and opportunity when it comes to managing emotions, and that body language can have more impact than words.

An international football head coach described his approach to me: "Touchline behaviour can spread fear instead of creativity and confidence." Efforts to get this right have led head coaches to seek third-party observations of their touchline behaviour, even during training. The head coach of a women's football team told me that "it's hugely important, and that's something I've worked on. I've asked people in to watch my sessions because people are sometimes frightened of me, and I don't want that."

An international hockey coach has taken things one step further. "I've been miked up for training sessions in order to reflect and chat to other coaches about it. It's something I'm very conscious of and I definitely don't get it right all the time. You want to display your values as much as you can. It's the same when I'm on the sideline, not showing the girls that I'm frustrated, and your body language alone can show that." He also keeps in mind the athletes not on the field of play. "If someone doesn't give the right pass, and you react . . . The bench sees you do that, and they are thinking, 'The next time I'm on the pitch in that situation, that's how he will react.' They won't want to disappoint you or get stuff wrong, then they don't try things. They might not try what they should have tried, and it's because of you. You've given a subliminal message."

An international volleyball coach told me he learned that he was too animated at courtside. "I was expressing my emotions too much. My body language on the sideline was shocking. I got someone I know to come and watch me and write a report on my behaviour, and that helped. He took some video footage too and went through that with me, and it was amazing to see . . . I've toned it down a lot as a result of that. The athletes need someone who seems to be in control and not too emotional in either direction."

The latter point about being perceived to be in control is important. Team members want to see a leader who is calm and who has the answers, not one who is panicking. A men's football head coach told me, "I took an exercise two seasons back where a coach mentor of mine came in and observed, firstly training and then a whole match day. One of the things he noticed was that the way you act or show yourself on the sideline can affect the players, and when times are tough and they see arms up on the bench, it just makes them more frustrated. So, if we are frustrated, they will be. If they look over and see a cool head and someone communicating clearly . . . Look, at the end of the day, we are human and there's always going to be someone with some emotions happening, but in the main they get a lot of positives from seeing someone in control and clear in their thinking."

An ice hockey head coach told me that "they know that I will help them find a way. I want them to see me as a source for solutions." Similarly, a hypothetical head coach who trots off confidently towards the changing room at half-time is subconsciously telling his team not to worry, and that he has some solutions. Before the team has reached the changing rooms, his players are already feeling more confident about the second half.

Projecting calm and control may be important; however, having learned from third-party observation, a lacrosse head coach found that he was holding too many emotions in, and that he displayed the consequences of that from time to time, when his pent-up frustrations escaped: "I spend so much time trying to keep quiet and not exhibiting negative body language, I do find that when I'm triggered, I really go off on one. That hasn't happened for a few years, fortunately."

The third-party observation strategy represents reflective practice, an important part of empathic leadership. An empathic leader is skilled in understanding other perspectives but is also open to advice from outside the group to help achieve this goal. However, a cricket head coach I spoke with is hesitant about this method. He told me, "I don't believe you can rely on second-hand information." What he means by this is that the third party is not one of the athletes, and therefore they may have a very different perspective to that of the athletes. The third party may employ empathy, mentalising, or perspective taking, to embrace the athlete's perspective; however, their levels of empathic accuracy will impact their success. Getting feedback from athletes may help. Even then, few people understand the true influences of behaviours on other people.

Empathic leaders are aware that the perceptions athletes have of them will impact performance. An ice hockey head coach said to me, "I've learned over time that, as a leader, my reactions are not viewed the same as a player's, and I still had a player's mentality when I started coaching. Now there are times when my reaction, not vocal, but a facial expression – well, there are times when I consciously ignore things. If you react bad all the time, it puts more unease in the players." For head coaches less able to manage their own reactions, it is better to keep a distance. This idea led one of the head coaches I met to take a seat in the stands. He explained that "you are less emotional in the stands. It's easy to be a bit more controlled and limit your negative influence."

A leader skilled in managing emotions is able to take things a step further. An ice hockey head coach told me, "There are times when I think we're too flat emotionally, then maybe I start screaming at the referee. It's something that I do consciously, most of the time. I think it helps when we need something to get going." The awareness of a team's emotions has to be continually updated throughout a game. Events during a game will alter athletes' emotional states. A women's football head coach told me, "We've had moments where goals are scored in quick succession. I've done some stuff around emotions, and they talked about emotions staying in your brain for two minutes, and the actual physical processes are ongoing for those two minutes, and until you get that out of your mind, you can't go again. That's why you are dangerous when you've just scored. I've spoken to my players about this and said that after we score, the next two minutes are really important. Or if something goes wrong. You need to regulate yourself, get that ecstasy, or whatever, out of your system, and get yourself focused again." This level of understanding will help to modify a head coach's touchline behaviour throughout the game.

Another football head coach simply said that "it is important for a head coach to be aware of the power of their behaviour". Contagious positive and negative displays of emotion projected through the head coach's touchline behaviour, or reactions in training, after a game, or at any other time, can have implications for the emotions of team members and therefore have an impact on performance and the safety of the team climate. An angry coach, jumping up and down on the touchline, may achieve little other than instilling a climate of fear in to his team, which will negatively impact its performance.

Team members are better helped by behaviour that is calm and where the leader looks in control. This is typical of empathic leadership behaviour, as it considers others' perspectives and the implications the behaviour will have. The head coach of an international lacrosse team told me that "the empathic style is expressed by a willingness to understand self and the impact on others". The impact on team members' emotions has significant consequences for the team climate, which ultimately determines the well-being and performance levels of all concerned. With an empathic approach, leaders have a greater chance of achieving and maintaining climate safety, and therefore high levels of performance and success.

Notes

1. Keatings, D. (2020). League Notes: British Gymnastics' "climate of fear is real," Dan Keatings says. *Sports Business Journal.* www.sportsbusinessdaily.com/ Global/Issues/2017/11/15/Leagues-and-Governing-Bodies/notes.aspx
2. PressFrom. (2020). UK Sport digesting "climate of fear" findings within British Para-Swimming. https://pressfrom.info/uk/news/sport/-215105-uk-sport-digesting-climate-of-fear-findings-within-british-para-swimming.html
3. Ashkanasy, N. & Nicholson, G. (2003). Climate of fear in organisational settings: Construct definition, measurement and a test of theory. *Australian Journal of Psychology, 55*(1), 24–29.
4. Holt, S. & Marques, J. (2012). Empathy in leadership: Appropriate or misplaced? An empirical study on a topic that is asking for attention. *Journal of Business Ethics, 105*, 95–105.
5. Phelps, A., Kelly, J., Lancaster, S., Mehrzad, J. & Panter, A. (2017). *Report of the Independent Review Panel into the Climate and Culture of the World Class Programme in British Cycling.* www.uksport.gov.uk/news/2017/06/14/british-cycling
6. Rumsby, B. (2017). British coach created "climate of fear" for disabled swimmers. *The Telegraph.* www.telegraph.co.uk/swimming/2017/10/12/british-coach-created-climate-fear-disabled-swimmers
7. Gómez-López, M., Borrego, C. C., da Silva, C. M., Granero-Gallegos, A. & González-Hernández, J. (2020). Effects of motivational climate on fear of failure and anxiety in teen handball players. *International Journal of Environmental Research and Public Health, 17*(2), 592.
8. Andrade, A., Batalha Silva, R. & Dominski, F. H. (2020). Application of sport psychology to mixed martial arts. *Kinesiology, 52*(1), 94–102.
9. Dasborough, M. T., Ashkanasy, N. M., Tee, E. Y. J. & Tse, H. H. M. (2009). What goes around comes around: How meso-level negative emotional contagion can ultimately determine organizational attitudes toward leaders. *Leadership Quarterly, 20*(4), 571–585.
10. Ashkanasy, N. M. & Humphrey, R. H. (2011). Current emotion research in organizational behavior. *Emotion Review, 3*(2), 214–224.
11. Edmondson, A. C. & Lei, Z. (2014). Psychological safety: The history, renaissance, and future of an interpersonal construct. *Annual Review of Organizational Psychology and Organizational Behavior, 1*, 23–43.

12. Tynan, R. (2005). The effects of threat sensitivity and face giving on dyadic psychological safety and upward communication. *Journal of Applied Social Psychology*, *35*(2), 223–247.

13. Rogers, C. & Roethlisberger, F. (1952). Barriers and gateways to communication. *Harvard Business Review*, July–August.

14. Rivera, J. De & De Rivera, J. (1992). Emotional climate: Social structure and emotional dynamics. In K. T. Strongman (Ed.), *International review of studies on emotion*, Vol. 2 (pp. 197–218). John Wiley & Sons.

15. Ruhl, S. & Ennker, J. (2012). Empathische Führung. *Zeitschrift für Herz-, Thorax- und Gefäßchirurgie*, *26*, 123–128.

16. Tzouramani, E. (2017). Leadership and empathy. In J. Marques & S. Dhiman (Eds), *Leadership today: Practices for personal and professional perfomance* (pp. 197–216). Springer. doi:10.1007/978-3-319-31036-7_11

17. Berry, D. H. & Joannidès, V. (2013). The source of empathy in our lives: An explanatory journey into the realm of spirituality. In K. Pavlovich & K. Krahnke (Eds), *Organizing through empathy* (pp. 34–48). Routledge.

18. Kock, N., Mayfield, M., Mayfield, J., Sexton, S. & De La Garza, L. M. (2019). Empathetic leadership: How leader emotional support and understanding influences follower performance. *Journal of Leadership and Organizational Studies*, *26*(2), 217–236.

19. Morelli, S. A., Lieberman, M. D. & Zaki, J. (2015). The emerging study of positive empathy. *Social and Personality Psychology Compass*, *9*(2), 57–68.

20. Andreychik, M. R. & Migliaccio, N. (2015). Empathizing with others' pain versus empathizing with others' joy: Examining the separability of positive and negative empathy and their relation to different types of social behaviors and social emotions. *Basic and Applied Social Psychology*, *37*(5), 274–291.

21. Main, A., Walle, E. A., Kho, C. & Halpern, J. (2017). The interpersonal functions of empathy: A relational perspective. *Emotion Review*, *9*(4), 358–366.

22. Duhigg, C. (2016). What Google learned from its quest to build the perfect team. *The New York Times*. www.nytimes.com/2016/02/28/magazine/what-google-learned-from-its-quest-to-build-the-perfect-team.html

23. Brenton, B. & Levin, D. (2012). The softer side of innovation: The people. *Journal of Product Innovation Management*, *29*(3), 364–366.

24. Lafley, A. & Charan, R. (2008). *The game-changer: How you can drive revenue and profit growth with innovation*. Portfolio/Penguin.

25. Amabile, T. M., Schatzel, E. A., Moneta, G. B. & Kramer, S. J. (2004). Leader behaviors and the work environment for creativity: Perceived leader support. *Leadership Quarterly*, *15*(1), 5–32.

26. Persson, B. N. & Kajonius, P. J. (2016). Empathy and universal values explicated by the empathy–altruism hypothesis. *Journal of Social Psychology*, *156*(6), 610–619.

27. Fry, M. D. & Gano-Overway, L. A. (2010). Exploring the contribution of the caring climate to the youth sport experience. *Journal of Applied Sport Psychology*, *22*(3), 294–304.

28. Noddings, N. (2010). *The maternal factor: Two paths to morality*. University of California Press.

29. Gano-Overway, L. A. (2013). The caring climate: How sport environments can develop empathy in young people. In K. Pavlovich & K. Krahnke (Eds), *Organizing through empathy* (pp. 166–183). Routledge.

30. Metz, T. & Gaie, J. B. R. (2010). The African ethic of *Ubuntu/Botho*: Implications for research on morality. *Journal of Moral Education*, *39*(3), 273–290.

31. McMillan, D. W. & Chavis, D. M. (1986). Sense of community: A definition and theory. *Journal of Community Psychology*, *14*(1), 6–23.

32. O'Neil, D. A. (2011). The value of emotional intelligence for high performance coaching: A commentary. *International Journal of Sports Science and Coaching*, *6*(3), 315–328.

33. Lynoe, N., Löfmark, R. & Thulesius, H. O. (2008). Teaching medical ethics: What is the impact of role models? Some experiences from Swedish medical schools. *Journal of Medical Ethics*, *34*(4), 315–316.

34. Simon, F. (2013). The influence of empathy in complaint handling: Evidence of gratitudinal and transactional routes to loyalty. *Journal of Retailing and Consumer Services*, *20*(6), 599–608.

35. Humphrey, R. H. (2002). The many faces of emotional leadership. *Leadership Quarterly*, *13*(5), 493–504.

36. Chadwick, S. (2009). From outside lane to inside track: Sport management research in the twenty-first century. *Managment Decision*, *47*(1), 191–203.

37. Ancelotti, C., Brady, C. & Forde, M. (2017). *Quiet leadership*. Portfolio/Penguin.

38. Schneider, R. C. (2013). Emotional intelligence: The overlooked component of sport leadership. *International Journal of Sport and Society*, *3*(3), 43–56.

39. Stein, S., Papadogiannis, P., Yip, J. & Sitarenios, G. (2009). Emotional intelligence of leaders: A profile of top executives. *Leadership and Organization Development Journal*, *30*(1), 87–101.

40. Polychroniou, P. V. (2009). Relationship between emotional intelligence and transformational leadership of supervisors. *Team Performance Management*, *15*(7/8), 343–356.

41. Walter, F., Cole, M. S. & Humphrey, R. H. (2011). Emotional intelligence: Sine qua non of leadership or folderol? *Academy of Management Perspectives*, *25*(1), 45–59.

42. Weinberger, L. A. (2009). Emotional intelligence, leadership style, and perceived leadership effectiveness. *Advances in Developing Human Resources*, *11*(6), 747–772.

43. Ramesh, V. (2013). Emotional intelligence in leadership: A conceptual review. *International Journal of Organizational Behavior and Management Perspectives*, *2*(1), 210–216.

44. Ashkanasy, N. M. & Dorris, A. D. (2017). Emotions in the workplace. *Annual Review of Organizational Psychology and Organizational Behavior*, *4*, 67–90.

45. Wetterauer, U. & Ruhl, S. (2011). Empathische Führung: Veränderung positiv gestalte [Empathic leadership: Shaping positive change]. *Der Urologe*, *50*, 1578–1583.

46. Wagstaff, C. & Hanton, S. (2017). Emotions in sport organizations. In C. Wagstaff & S. Hanton (Eds), *The organizational psychology of sport* (pp. 33–61). Routledge.

47. de Rivera, J. & Páez, D. (2007). Emotional climate, human security, and cultures of peace. *Journal of Social Issues*, *63*(2), 233–253.

48. Yurtsever, G. & de Rivera, J. (2010). Measuring the emotional climate of an organization. *Perceptual and Motor Skills*, *110*(2), 501–516.

49. Gibb, J. R. (1961). Defensive communication. *Journal of Communication*, *11*(3), 141–148.

50. Hatfield, E., Rapson, R. L. & Le, L. (2013). Emotional contagion and empathy. In J. Decety & W. Ickes (Eds), *The social neuroscience of empathy* (pp. 19–30). MIT Press. doi:10.7551/mitpress/9780262012973.003.0003

51. Cuff, B. M. P., Brown, S. J., Taylor, L. & Howat, D. J. (2016). Empathy: A review of the concept. *Emotion Review*, *8*(2), 144–153.

52. Pate, L. & Shoblom, T. L. (2013). The ACES decision-making technique as a reframing tool for increasing empathy. In K. Pavlovich & K. Krahnke (Eds), *Organizing through empathy* (pp. 142–157). Routledge. doi:10.4324/978020 3754030-17

53. Riggio, R. E. & Reichard, R. J. (2008). The emotional and social intelligences of effective leadership. *Journal of Managerial Psychology*, *23*(2), 169–185.

54. Martin, D. & Heineberg, Y. (2018). Positive leadership, power and compassion. In P. Gilbert (Ed.), *Compassion: Concepts, research and applications* (pp. 221–236). Routledge. https://doi.org/10.4324/9781315564296-13

55. Colfax, R. S., Rivera, J. J. & Perez, K. T. (2010). Applying emotional intelligence (EQ-I) in the workplace: Vital to global business success. *Journal of International Business Research*, *9*, 89–98.

56. Kohlrieser, G., Goldsworthy, S. & Coombe, D.(2012). *Care to dare: Unleashing astonishing potential through secure base leadership*. Jossey-Bass.

57. Ioannidou, F., Konstantikaki, V., Ioannidou F & Konstantikaki V. (2008). Empathy and emotional intelligence: What is it really about? *International Journal of Caring Sciences*, *1*(3), 118–12.

58. Northouse, P. G. (2015). *Leadership: Theory and practice*. Sage Publications.

Person-Centred Focus   **5**

This may seem obvious, but it is worth repeating: athletes are people. They are individual human beings who perform as athletes. They are not shirt numbers, squad numbers, or pawns. Objectification is not good for them, you as their leader, or your team's performance. It is the same in all industries. To get the best out of each team member, you need to treat each of them as a unique human being. An empathic leader is a servant leader who understands and serves the needs of each team member.

Each of us has our own experiences and current life situations. An empathic leader is proactive about getting to know everything they can about the experiences and situations of each member of their team. Team members need to feel that they matter, that they are listened to, that their wellbeing is valued, and that their future is important to their leader and the club or organisation that they represent. These efforts not only empower the leader with greater knowledge but also encourage a sense of perceived empathy in everyone, which brings with it greater commitment and higher levels of performance.

Research has documented a change in the focus of leadership. Since the beginning of the twenty-first century, leadership across industries has been evolving from job-centred to worker-centred, and this has altered the role of leaders.[11] Worker-centred leadership entails leadership behaviours that develop mutual trust, respect, and empathy for workers. This approach not only emphasises a deeper concern for the needs of workers but also includes them in decision making. This worker-centred approach has progressed in elite sport. A rugby union head coach told me that "what is best for the person is best for the athlete".

DOI: 10.4324/9781003324676-6

The Athlete-Centred Approach

There has been a trend in elite sport from coach-centred to athlete-centred leadership.[2] Athlete-centred leadership focuses on greater trust, inclusion, and empathic concern for the athlete, while also providing opportunities for their empowerment and contribution.[3] Rather than making assumptions, head coaches learn about the unique character of each athlete, which allows athletes a greater role in their own development.

Although this athlete-centred approach to leadership is now dominating elite sport, one head coach warned that some leaders are being left behind. He told me that he believes that "there are plenty of people out there who just don't have a true understanding of what that means, or maybe don't even have a clear idea of what their own coaching philosophy is, or they do but their actual behaviour doesn't always match that philosophy". This last point is relevant to all leadership philosophy: it must be practised, not just preached.

By focusing on athletes as human beings, more genuine relationships develop, which improves trust and appreciation. Since they care about the perspectives of team members, empathic leaders appreciate being appreciated, and this can yield more influence when trying to modify behaviour. An international rugby union head coach described one such situation: "I sat down in a meeting with two of my younger players once and said to one of them, 'I know you don't want to be here.' He said, 'No, no I don't.' I said, 'I know you don't, you're an entertainer. The last place you want to be is in here, you want to be out on the pitch. I understand that. Yeah, I know you hate this meeting environment, but I know you love being out on that pitch. We'll give you that, but you have to engage with us here. I understand what floats your boat.'" Once assured of this understanding, a team member is more likely to be committed to the head coach.

Commitment is further enhanced when team members feel a sense of empowerment, when they feel trusted or consulted during decision making.[4] This is becoming more common and has other advantages, as a rugby union head coach explained to me: "We involve athletes in decisions that impact on them. We want to know what they think. And that also helps them to become decision makers on the pitch."

Treating athletes individually means letting them make their own decisions whenever possible. An ice hockey coach told me how he has enacted this in pre-game situations: "Back in the day, it was almost obligatory to have a pre-game skate in the morning of an evening game, but studies showed it doesn't give you anything physically – you are actually wasting energy. And . . . the guys, many of them were used to it and needed it, so many times we decided to make it optional: if you want to skate, do so; if not, don't. Then we had a lot of criticism saying we were being too soft on them. I got the guys together and said, 'Think about it: if I make you skate and you're not ready for the game, then it's down to me. Now it's on you; you know what gets you ready for the game. If you skate, fine; if you don't, I don't care. But you have to be ready at 7pm so whatever is easier for you.'"

An international head coach provided another good example of empowering rather than ruling his athletes: "Here's another example of empathy: a problem with drinking, going back a number of years – you know, a bit like boys on tour, get smashed, get up and play a game. We were mindful of that. In 2010, we told the players they had a two-beer limit. They went out, had their two beers and they wanted more beers, and because they'd been told, it becomes 'I can't have, therefore I want.' There was climbing out of dorm windows and crawling under windows to go out for more beers. In 2014, we started moving away from that and there was some better behaviour, but still probably stuff going on that us coaches didn't know about. In 2018, it's like the elephant in the room – 'What's the coach going to do?' My assistant coaches have been through this world; they said, 'Just tell them they can't drink.' But I said, 'You know what, I think that will create more problems.' We are then at the World Championships when our national football team, get through to the World Cup semi-final, and we are going out together to watch the game. I told my assistants the decision I was going to make, and they'd all bought into it, and we'd had discussions about it. I got the captain down and said, 'Look, we are going out to a bar.' It was the easiest place to watch the game together. I think this is where empathy came in. I said, 'Right, we are going to drink if we want to drink; it's not going to be a two-drinks rule. You know how hard the World Championships is going to be . . . You make the decision; you discuss it as a group and decide what you want to do.' So we go down to this bar, and there was a cultural shift in the group, and the benefits of this process of watching the game together was the players were drinking water; one or two maybe had another beer, but nobody had more than two beers. I'm pretty sure that if we had given them a two-pint limit, people would have had more than two pints. The fact that we told them nobody is going to be looking over their shoulder with a tally chart of beers drunk, none of that – a very different approach."

Close relationships allow empathic leaders to know people well enough to make good decisions about when to empower them, but sometimes it's a matter of empowering them with explanations. A football head coach told me what he might say to one of his athletes: "'I want you to play this way because it will improve you as a player, the team will function better, you'll be able to shine more.' I think any coach is somewhat set in their ways in terms of playing style, and so it's the conversation that's important, the explanation so that the players understand. It's not right just to say what they have to do and end the conversation there."

The understanding of individuals typical of empathic leaders is not restricted to their lives at work. An ice hockey head coach told me, "The greatest joy I get from leading the team isn't when we've won a championship or other things; it's when a former player calls when they need help with projects, like the one you are doing. I had a former player who is at university, and she called and asked me to participate in her work because she knew how I am as a person. And that's more rewarding than on-ice success. When you're empathic to the players and they know you care for them, it's going to mean more in life than what sports do for you."

Another ice hockey head coach told me a similar story: "I find the biggest achievements of my coaching career came at the beginning when I coached kids: a 15-year-old kid was 100kg and a lost soul. He couldn't socialise and he was just a big guy who couldn't find his way. And we managed to make him become an athlete, a better guy who has a better relationship with himself. He made his body into the one he wanted. I saw him with a girlfriend. He quit hockey – he was a terrible hockey player – but I saw him living the life he wanted to live." When team members understand how invested their leader is in each member of the team, their trust and commitment levels towards them grow.

A rugby union head coach told me that his role has "become far more athlete-centred now, than ever before, which suits empathic people". An international lacrosse head coach described his experience: "I have seen a change. You are seeing messages coming out of the highest-profile sports, about having an understanding of the person." This offers more than what you gain from athletes. Studies have shown that an athlete-centred approach improves a leader's job satisfaction[5] and boosts a team's performance.[6] It also alters the leader's reputation.

In the current era of elite sport, athletes have the power to seek out and maintain positions with coaches they trust and who make them feel understood and empowered. In this respect, any leader who serves such needs will better attract and retain talent, which offers a significant advantage in any sport. This principle applies in other industries too. The reputation of a leader has never been more powerful.

Perceived Empathy

Recognising the needs of individuals is one thing, but it is only when team members notice a leader's efforts to serve those needs that they begin to feel they are valued. By empathising with athletes, a head coach can enhance their understanding of what their life is like and consider how things could improve and what the potential is going forward. An athlete will notice an empathic approach.

Studies have shown that perceived empathy[7] alone enhances commitment.[8] A hockey head coach told me, "Empathy brings you closer, closer means more empathy, and that means more commitment: I think the biggest thing is it creates a willingness for players to play for you as a coach. Although I don't necessarily like the expression, I think they feel more *connected* to you as a member of the team rather than an authority figure."

The close relationships typical of empathic leadership bring vital information about exactly how to continue to improve commitment. A men's ice hockey head coach explained how his relationships help to gain commitment. He said that the idea is to "be curious, ask open-ended questions and then just sit back and listen, time allowing, of course. It helps me find ways of keeping them interested and motivated and feeling important; when you do that, they'll do whatever for you."

The commitment levels of athletes in elite sport have been complicated in recent years, with some athletes focusing on their own brand rather than the team's performance. An international hockey head coach told me, "We had one guy who scored a hat-trick and was all over social media and the rest of the players were thinking, 'Yeah, but we lost.' The boys came to me and said, 'Have you seen this?' That showed a real lack of empathy and was unacceptable. So I called him up and said, 'Look, can you see how this looks?'"

Changes in society and technology have thrown up a multitude of complexities, particularly when it comes to social media. The head coach of a women's football team explained to me: "You have lots of players who gear everything towards their profile on social media. It very much feels like all the 90 minutes was about was how people will see them from the outside world. The person they are projecting is seen by ten thousand people, say, and there were only a thousand at the game. They can get ten thousand approvals." Only by gaining understanding through close relationships with team members will a leader know how to communicate why prioritising social media is detrimental for the team and the athlete personally. Empathic leaders know how to explain to team members that their behaviour has consequences and that what they do online matters. More than this, empathic leaders will ensure team members feel that they themselves matter.

Anyone who is confident that they have meaningful and positive connections with others will feel that they matter.[9] This centres on the power of feeling valued.[9] A person who feels they matter is someone who feels important, visible, and listened to, while the person who feels as though he or she does not matter feels unimportant, invisible, and unheard.[10] Once a team member understands that they matter, they realise that they have been recognised by a leader and understood for who they are.

A leader will find it more difficult to gain understanding of individuals who are putting on an act or playing a role in the workplace. It is not good for the individual either. As a cricket head coach told me, "If they play a role, it's draining for them. That will impact on their wellbeing and their performance." When I met this head coach at his club's ground, he went on to illustrate how important it is to make each person feel accepted, not just by their head coach, but also their teammates: "Actually, spending time with them, out of this environment is important to me. We had one young player who, in the dressing room, was basically on mute. He didn't offer anything. But he had this swagger about him; there was something. I thought there's more to this guy. Then one day the lads came in and said, 'Oh, you should've seen this guy last night, he was amazing!' It was like two different people. It turned out he was a massive dancer, like a proper dancer. I caught him in the gym, dancing in his pants. I said, 'What do you think you're doing?' He looked at me. I said, 'Look, I love this, it's who you are. And so this is who you need to be when you're here.' Interestingly, a lot of the others had assumed he was aloof, arrogant, whatever. He went twelfth man to a first-team game and behaved true to himself, and by the end of the trip the lads loved him, they absolutely loved him."

Athletes want to be seen, heard, and understood as who they are. They need to have the freedom to be their genuine selves. In the words of an international football head coach, "They need to know that you appreciate them for who they are rather than just what they are." Once a leader understands who they are, they can adjust their leadership practices appropriately. This won't always entail an approach that feels warm.

A football head coach in Australia told me, "Some need a kick up the arse, and know that's what they need: they *want* a kick up the arse. So you can't be too fluffy with them. You need to be empathic to understand what you need to do."

While the goal of the empathic leader is to determine the needs of each individual athlete, and this can be very unique, a cricket head coach told me that he refers to Maslow's Hierarchy of Needs[11] as a reminder of the kind of things to be aware of. Paraphrasing, the head coach concisely reminded me of the five elements of Maslow's model: "So you have well-being at the bottom, then safety, belonging, self-esteem or self-respect, and self-actualisation at the top. This last stage is very important; it's about me as a leader helping an athlete to become who they can become. When I'm learning more about my players, one of these stages usually resonates."

Prioritising individuals goes against the adage of the team coming first. I asked an international volleyball head coach how this can make sense. He told me, "I try to put the person before the athlete, before the team even. That's not easy to understand, so let me explain. The team is the most important thing. To get the best from the team, my job is to make sure each component, each person within it is performing to their best ability. To do that, I have to make sure they are okay on a human level. If everything in their life is going well and they feel supported and cared for, if they feel I understand them and their perspective, then they are more likely to give their best for the team, and so I'm doing my job for the team by doing my job for the individual. Hope that makes sense?" It does make sense. If an athlete perceives support, care, understanding, and empathy, they are bound to be more committed.

This support, care, understanding, and empathy can be demonstrated throughout a working week in elite sport. For away games, athletes may feel a little more stressed than for home games, due to unfamiliar surroundings. Efforts to make surroundings more familiar can help. Whether they do or not, the efforts will be noticed and appreciated. Typically, such efforts involve putting up posters of the players in action or team colours on the walls; music players and any other items that can be brought into the dressing room can all help to make athletes feel more at home. I asked a netball head coach what plans she has for away changing rooms. "We make it ours," she said. "And our players appreciate it."

A women's football head coach works similarly. He reminded me of other needs that can be served in these moments. "With the national team, we have people go in early and put their shirts out and make them feel at home a bit. It's like we've made an effort. But before they go out to warm up, we make the players aware of what a ground is like from a player's perspective: if you're right up against the crowd, if it's likely to be hostile. Making them aware in that sense is key. It stops them freezing."

At training each day, an empathic leader will still be focusing on understanding the needs of a group even when they are not obvious to others. A men's football head coach told me the following story: "One day last year, we were first in the league, but I could sense there was over-confidence, and they were getting a bit lackadaisical. We started doing some technical stuff, and balls were going all over the place, under people's feet. People weren't connecting with ten-yard passes. I decided to stop the session and send them home. My assistants looked at me, but I just said, 'Go home, clear your heads. If your heads are not clear tomorrow, you won't train, and you need to consider what it means being a professional footballer.' The next day, the training session was great. We ended up winning 5–1 at the weekend. I don't know if that was the reason, but I think understanding your players enables you to act in a certain way. I felt it needed to happen." I asked what information is most useful in making such drastic decisions, and he told me, "Body language – you can spot things as soon as they walk out on the training field, you can see straight away where their heads are at. Some are different – they are laughing and joking and in a good place. Some take a while to get into it. I always tell them what we are going to do and why we are doing it at the start of training, and I can read what they think of that when I say it. That's a starting point of my understanding of how they feel." The nuances of body language are unique to each individual.[12] The skill of recognising these nuances is enhanced by building closer relationships.[13]

For ambitious leaders in any industry, it is tempting to take shortcuts to knowing and understanding team members. Why put in all that time and effort if you can use psychological tests and profiling? An international rugby union head coach told me that while they still do this, it is no substitute for human connection. He said, "By spending time with each other, with other coaches too, you get to understand them, and it shapes how you address them because you know you will get different responses from different people if you go at it in the same way. If you are dealing with an empathic-type person, and you are very direct, like me, I have to think about not putting them in a spin. I need to sit down and discuss it more carefully. Delivering messages in the right way ensures they stay engaged, and it can only be done through knowing them, not from test scores."

The head coach of an international football team explained to me that while "there are lots of psychological tools, a closer relationship helps you understand people better, you get to find out about family issues, and you get to learn how they deal with stress *et cetera*. Sometimes a player might act very calm and cool, and yet I know behind the scenes it's a shitshow at home." The head coach of an international lacrosse team agreed, saying, "All leaders will want their team members to be in the right frame of mind for the tasks ahead. Understanding their motivations, their triggers, their challenges, what works for them inside the sport and what's going on for them outside of the sport. Those are the sort of things. In the approach that I take these days, empathy becomes a vital component of trying to understand them as people and as athletes."

Wellbeing

Worker wellbeing is more of a concern now than ever before. It has been shown to influence performance, staff turnover, and customer loyalty.[14] It is not only the worker or athlete who profits: empathy in the workplace generates positive emotional states for leaders too.[15] An empathic leader will have a greater awareness of their own wellbeing and that of others, and this awareness can inform their behaviour and decision making. This may involve a change in the empathiser's emotional state caused by forecasting feelings in the other. For example, a hockey head coach told me that when news about a scandal was about to break concerning one of the staff, he thought about the impact on the athletes. He explained to me that he thought, "I know how they're going to feel about this when they find out."[16] This forecasting ability may allow a leader to protect individuals and themselves. Leader empathy not only helps workplace wellbeing but also increases a team member's job satisfaction.[17]

Job satisfaction has become a priority as leadership has become more worker-centred. Job satisfaction is influenced by the way the worker sees their leader.[18] When they see that the leader supports them, their satisfaction is enhanced.[6] There is usually a gap between how team members want a leader to be and how they actually are.[1] This gap provides an opportunity to increase job satisfaction and subsequently performance.[6] Job satisfaction will also influence organisational commitment,[19] trust, and engagement.[20]

Engaged, elite athletes are typically strong-minded, resilient, confident, composed, and focused individuals. However, they are no less susceptible to mental illness than the rest of us.[21] Cases of elite sports performers suffering from depression, anxiety, eating disorders, obsessive compulsive disorders, addictions, substance misuse, and burnout appear in the media regularly.[22] A leader lacking empathy is more likely to overlook the signs. Being highly attuned to others' moods and emotions is a vital aspect of understanding what other people are experiencing.

At some point, leaders must make decisions that they know will have a negative impact on team members, and subsequent feelings of guilt can become draining. Self-regulation, where empathic behaviours are monitored and controlled, can help to suppress the negative consequences of this guilt.[23] Identifying ways to regulate and cope with these unpleasant emotions is fundamental to a leader's own wellbeing.[24]

During high-stress moments, cortisol modifies our behaviour by sending a signal to indicate that a challenging situation needs to be resolved. It is when a situation remains unresolved that cortisol levels begin to have a significant impact: increasing blood sugar, suppressing immunity, inhibiting bone growth, and even increasing healing time.[25, 26] In elite sport, this could relate to a poor run of form, an injury, a contract negotiation, or a particularly difficult relationship.

By showing understanding, a leader can reduce stress, increasing oxytocin and reducing cortisol levels. This encourages cooperation and bonding, as well as improving athlete wellbeing. A leader's understanding can be facilitated by drawing on their own experiences and potentially sharing them with a team member in need. This is usually well received, as an international rugby union head coach confirmed: "I've shared stuff about my own life, and I can tell they appreciate it."

Empathic leaders maintain concern about the lives of team members away from work. When someone is struggling with grief, their leader's experiences can be of help. An international lacrosse head coach said, "I've lost people, I know how they're feeling. I mean not exactly, but I share my experience with them, and then they believe I care, you know." Similarly, an international volleyball head coach told me, "I've been through a serious illness and a divorce and so I have a fair bit of life experience, which can prove invaluable. Just by sharing those things with a player, they feel you trust them with that and so they should trust you with stuff and they open up. I sometimes have to remind them it's just a game, you know. Life is not just about volleyball. You need to show you care for them. It's a dangerous situation for a coach if a player thinks they have no empathy."

Expressing empathy in a situation is more challenging when the leader has no relevant life experiences to draw on. An international handball head coach told me, "I had a player, a young player of 16, and she was self-harming. She was a very talented player and important to the squad. I had to strip things back and see things from her point of view and the effect it was having on her as an athlete and her as a person too." Where experience is lacking, the imaginative skill of mentalising or cognitive empathy becomes a necessary tool.[27]

As an international football head coach told me, "Life events are now accepted by elite head coaches to be bigger than their sport." A rugby union head coach told me, "It means looking out for them in their wider lives, preparing them for life after rugby; it means helping them with their education, working experience. It also means looking out for their families as well. That doesn't mean to say you know about everything that's going on, so what we do with the staff is that as a coaching group we allocate players to a coach who we think has the best chance of understanding that player, who has a rapport with that player."

Sometimes a leader may be better off delegating to another member of staff who has experienced what a team member is going through, but whoever it is, the connection in these moments is a powerful one. One head coach shared the following with me: "I had two brothers in the team that I was coaching and one of those brothers passed away tragically. And to deal with that at a coaching level is, to my mind, entirely missing the point. There is nothing more personal or human than bereavement. When it's a sibling who shares your passion for the same sport and is at the same level as you, there are so many more things going into that, which simply transcends just coaching. Being respectful of that player's needs and being respectful and understanding of how that would impact him as an athlete. His best friend asked for time away from the sport. One response would be: this is elite level sport, it's a competitive environment, there'll be someone ready to take your place. Time away from the sport was sure to have an impact. Myself, and the rest of the staff, decided that wasn't the way to go, either at a human level, a coach level, and that a more empathic approach was to tell him to take time away and the ball's in your court as to when you return to the group. He did that, came back, and captained the team really effectively, but on reflection it's easy to see how another approach could have been justified, but we thought that a more empathic approach would prove beneficial."

Mental health issues have become more common, and athletes are more likely to admit to having them if they perceive their leader to be empathic.[28] They won't approach a leader who is cold and autocratic. Their fear would be a lack of understanding or being dropped from the team. I asked an experienced international head coach how something like this would be viewed by a leader of 20 years ago, and she said, "It may have been seen as weakness." This reaction is less likely in the modern era when leaders have realised it will have a negative impact on their leadership goals and the team's pursuit of sustainable success. The head coach of a women's football team told me, "If they feel anxious, I try to understand the severity of that. In the younger players in particular, it's a fairly common occurrence now. I have to understand what they are going through, and the girls trust me to do that, I think."

An international football head coach agreed with this approach, saying, "I think trust is vital. You need to be clear these issues will stay between us, maybe another staff member, until they are comfortable to release it. Always, what you are telling me stays here and I will support you. For example, I think we had a situation where there was a substance abuse issue. He felt he didn't have a problem, but that others felt he had a problem. We both knew that if it continued to be reported, it would be a problem whether he had a problem or not. We got him to the point that he admitted maybe he did have a problem; we said, 'You've obviously done something for these people to think this, so we need you to go away and think about it. We are here to support you, but we need you to go and think about this and think about what steps are necessary going forward.' He came back and said that maybe he needed to have someone look at him to decide if he has a problem. And we helped him from there."

These examples represent very delicate situations that require careful and considered responses. The benefits to leadership stretch further than the individual team member. Head coaches in elite sport understand that their athletes are watching them all of the time and judging their reactions when they go to them with issues, but as an international rugby union head coach told me, "It's not just the athlete with the issue, but the rest of the squad will be judging too. If you can have players telling other players, 'Look, go see the coach, he's all right, he'll listen to you,' that's powerful and something I keep working on, breaking down the barrier really, so that they don't worry about coming to me."

It's not always a matter of the team member approaching their leader, or of something being flagged up by a teammate or the media. One international head coach explained how aware a leader must be and then how careful they must be with the approach. He told me, "We had a strong player, very successful, but it had been determined by ourselves and our medical staff that he might have a learning disability that had been undetected through his youth. No guarantees, and we had to make sure that when we sat down to talk to him, he understood that the medical staff was there to help him and support him. We had to imagine how critical and devastating it could be for him to find something out like this. He might immediately think, 'Oh my god, my career is over.' It wasn't that serious, but if we didn't get him to start working on it, it could have been a problem. The advice was that we will get you a deeper medical inspection so that we can get the best help for you. You can imagine that became less about sport and more about him . . . And it was very challenging."

Maintaining the wellbeing of team members is not always as complicated as the incident just described. Sometimes it can be about relationship breakdowns, which is a common experience and likely to be one the head coach has gone through. A football head coach explained this to me: "I've had men athletes approach me who've split up with their girlfriends, and I know what that's like. Trust me, I've been there." As people get older, get married, and have children, their relationship breakdowns become more complex and damaging. Another head coach told me, "It's difficult. If there are kids involved and it's a divorce, it's a hard one to deal with. Maybe fortunately for us, that usually happens when athletes are finished playing and start getting on their partner's nerves! I wouldn't wish it on anyone, obviously. I've only had two divorces with athletes of ours over a 20-year period. I hope that's it. Sometimes you just don't know what to say to them if I'm honest. All I can do is listen and see if I can help."

Such events in the personal lives of team members are likely to impact performance. Empathic leaders are likely to notice when something isn't right, and they know that they must initiate a conversation if athletes are being distracted by events at home, as an international football head coach explained to me: "It was at a point when it's not right and I had to say, 'Look, maybe you need to take a day or two to go and spend time with your family,' and boom! Right away, they say, 'Oh, really?' 'Absolutely, because if your family isn't right, you're not right and then you're no good to me, so go sort it out.'" I asked what the reaction was from the athlete after things had calmed down. He told me it was "an increased appreciation, increased attention, and understanding. It's 'Thanks, you were looking out for me and, by the way, I'll be looking out for you now. I'm going to be working harder and do what you want me to do.' Every now and then, you get one who just thinks, 'Great, I got a day off,' but generally it's far more than that. Maybe it's when I don't select that player and his reaction then is less aggressive. He's thinking, 'Wait a minute, this guy supported me and cares about me.'"

Empathic leaders cultivate relationships where team members are confident and trusting enough to come forward when they have a problem of any kind, without fearing the consequences. A cricket head coach told me, "I'm constantly on at the guys about being honest. I want them to come to me and go, you know, 'I'm feeling shit, I'm struggling,' and this could be a day before a game. I'll say okay, but they won't do it, they'll think you'll leave them out. I'll say, 'It's my job to make sure you are ready for this game, so we now have 12 hours to get you ready. I'm not dropping you. I may drop you in two weeks' time if we are in the same position, but my job is to help you. But if I don't know something and you're going, "I'm fine," and I know in my gut you're not going to perform, and the cricket tells us that.'"

Whether driven by the implications for performance or responsibility, elite sports organisations have made athlete wellbeing a priority, as a rugby union head coach explained to me: "The simple contract we have with our players, outside of their playing contract, is we said that the club is going to treat you unbelievably well; it means lots of things, the best expertise, the best support we can give them from a performance point of view. It also means looking out for them in their wider lives."

Empathic leaders focus on the person before the athlete. Their investment in personal growth as well as progression in the sport is noticed by the athlete. This noticing, exemplifies perceived empathy, and it leads to improved levels of trust, commitment, and performance.

Notes

1. Boatwright, K. J. & Forrest, L. (2000). Leadership preferences: The influence of gender and needs for connection on workers' ideal preferences for leadership behaviors. *Journal of Leadership Studies*, 7(2), 18–34.
2. Milbrath, M. (2017). Athlete-centered coaching: What, why, and how. *Track Coach, 218,* 6939–6944.
3. Kidman, L., Hadfield, D. & Thorpe, R. (2010). *Athlete-centred coaching: Developing inspired and inspiring people.* IPC Print Resources.
4. Kidman, L. & Lombardo, B. J. (2005). *Athlete-centred coaching: Developing decision makers.* IPC Print Resources.
5. Jowett, S. & Poczwardowski, A. (2007). Understanding the coach–athlete relationship. In S. Jowett & D. Lavallee (Eds), *Social Psychology in Sport* (pp. 3–14). Human Kinetics.
6. Amabile, T. M., Schatzel, E. A., Moneta, G. B. & Kramer, S. J. (2004). Leader behaviors and the work environment for creativity: Perceived leader support. *Leadership Quarterly*, 15(1), 5–32.
7. Woodall, W. G. & Hill, S. E. K. (1982). Predictive and perceived empathy as predictors of leadership style. *Perceptual and Motor Skills*, 54(3), 800–802.
8. Joireman, J., Daniels, D., George-Falvy, J. & Kamdar, D. (2006). Organizational citizenship behaviors as a function of empathy, consideration of future consequences, and employee time horizon: An initial exploration using an in-basketsimulation of OCBs. *Journal of Applied Social Psychology*, 36(9), 2266–2292.
9. Ghaye, T., Allen, L. & Clark, N. (2021). The holistic wellbeing of elite youth performers: U MATTER. In N. Campbell, A. Brady & A. Tincknell-Smith (Eds), *Developing and supporting athlete wellbeing: Person first, athlete second* (pp. 18–32). Routledge.

10. Flett, G. L. (2022). An introduction, review, and conceptual analysis of mattering as an essential construct and an essential way of life. *Journal of Psychoeducational Assessment, 40*(1), 3–36.

11. Maslow, A. H. (1943). A theory of human motivation. *Psychological Review, 50*(4), 370–396.

12. Barrett, L. F. (2017). *How emotions are made: The secret life of the brain.* Macmillan.

13. Lanzoni, S. (2018). *Empathy: A history.* Yale University Press.

14. Krekel, C., Ward, G. & De Neve, J.-E. (2019). Employee wellbeing, productivity, and firm performance. *SSRN Electronic Journal.* doi:10.2139 / ssrn.3356581

15. Boyatzis, R. E., Smith, M. L. & Blaize, N. (2006). Developing sustainable leaders through coaching and compassion. *Academy of Management Learning and Education, 5*(1), 8–24.

16. Redmond, M. V. (1989). The functions of empathy (decentering) in human relations. *Human Relations, 42*(7), 593–605.

17. Kock, N., Mayfield, M., Mayfield, J., Sexton, S. & De La Garza, L. M. (2019). Empathetic leadership: How leader emotional support and understanding influences follower performance. *Journal of Leadership and Organizational Studies, 26*(2), 217–236.

18. Zampetakis, L. A. & Moustakis, V. (2011). Managers' trait emotional intelligence and group outcomes: The case of group job satisfaction. *Small Group Research, 42*(1), 77–102.

19. Moorman, R. H., Niehoff, B. P. & Organ, D. W. (1993). Treating employees fairly and organizational citizenship behavior: Sorting the effects of job satisfaction, organizational commitment, and procedural justice. *Employee Responsibilities and Rights Journal, 6*(3), 209–225.

20. Gruman, J. A. & Saks, A. M. (2011). Performance management and employee engagement. *Human Resource Management Review, 21*(2), 123–136.

21. Gulliver, A., Griffiths, K. M. & Christensen, H. (2012). Barriers and facilitators to mental health help-seeking for young elite athletes: A qualitative study. *BMC Psychiatry, 12*, 157.

22. Larkin, D., Levy, A. R., Marchant, D. & Martin, C. R. (2017). When winners need help: Mental health in elite sport. *The Psychologist*, August, 42–46.

23. Cameron, C. D. & Payne, B. K. (2011). Escaping affect: How motivated emotion regulation creates insensitivity to mass suffering. *Journal of Personality and Social Psychology, 100*(1), 1–15.

24. Burch, G., Bennett, A., Humphrey, R., Batchelor, J. & Cairo, A. (2016). Unraveling the complexities of empathy research: A multi-level model of empathy in organizations. In *Research on Emotion in Organizations* vol. 12 (pp. 169–189). Emerald Group Publishing.

25. Ebrecht, M., Hextall, J., Kirtley, L.-G., Taylor, A., Dyson, M. & Weinman, J. (2004). Perceived stress and cortisol levels predict speed of wound healing in healthy male adults. *Psychoneuroendocrinology*, *29*(6), 798–80.

26. Ekstrand, J., Lundqvist, D., Lagerbäck, L., Vouillamoz, M., Papadimitiou, N. & Karlsson, J. (2018). Is there a correlation between coaches' leadership styles and injuries in elite football teams? A study of 36 elite teams in 17 countries. *British Journal of Sports Medicine*, *52*(8), 527–531.

27. Gilin, D., Maddux, W. W., Carpenter, J. & Galinsky, A. D. (2013). When to use your head and when to use your heart: The differential value of perspective-taking versus empathy in competitive interactions. *Personality and Social Psychology Bulletin*, *39*(1), 3–16.

28. O'Malley, A. L. & Gregory, J. B. (2011). Don't be such a downer: Using positive psychology to enhance the value of negative feedback. *Psychologist-Manager Journal*, *14*(4), 247–264.

Empathic Accuracy   6

Empathic accuracy is defined as an ability to precisely understand the specific content of another's thoughts and feelings.[1] Such intimate knowledge of other people has been shown to be invaluable in leadership.[2] In elite sport, this knowledge allows a head coach to predict an athlete's actions.[3] The close relationships typical of empathic leadership allow a leader to collect enough information to be able to predict the behaviour of a team member. This is achieved by empathising with them in an imagined context. In elite sport, this means understanding how an athlete will react when put into a particular situation. This knowledge will inform leadership actions including selection, communication, and task appropriation.[4]

A deep understanding of the inner world of an individual also hands a leader a more informed picture of the potential of that individual. This information will then help with recruitment and retention decisions. It's not merely about an empathic leader's own team members. Empathy can be employed to predict the strategy of rivals or to understand their fears and strengths. The more a leader knows their rival, the more accurately they will be able to imagine their inner world. Empathic skills offer a leader a method of data collection that will give them a huge advantage.

By collating snippets of information known as impression cues, or inferences, leaders form unique pictures of team members.[5] These impression cues are derived from the team member's performance, appearance, attitude, and behaviour. It is important that impression cues are kept up to date in order to maintain the leader's empathic accuracy. Empathic leaders then develop an expectancy of those team members based on these impression cues. This moulds the way a leader will interact with a team member and the decisions made concerning them. The information can be utilised

DOI: 10.4324/9781003324676-7

to help with anything from managing conflict to managing expectations. In elite sport, this can change everything from the way training sessions are set out to who is selected to take penalty kicks.

A head coach observing an athlete or group of athletes fidgeting and disengaged in training can decide to move on to something else, and then come back to it later. The more the leader knows a team member, the more information they will be able to collate through observing dialogue, body language, and performance. A talented athlete may perform with his head down, and a head coach who doesn't know him might believe he is lacking confidence, whereas a head coach who knows him well understands that it is just his personal style and doesn't reflect his mood.

Empathic accuracy is considered vital in the heat of action.[6] In elite sport, the athletes do their most important work while performing. The head coach is sidelined and left to make judgements based on body language and actions that are unique to each individual. It is no good for a head coach or their team if they get these judgements wrong; they must be correct in their perceptions. This can only be achieved through the levels of familiarity that stem from close relationships. A list of characteristics determined from psychometric tools will never be enough. A head coach needs to gain a depth of understanding that enables them to notice specific behaviours and then comprehend what it means when each team member displays such behaviours.

To maintain this ability, leaders should be regularly asking themselves what they think a team member is feeling in any moment and trying to empathise with their position to deepen that understanding. Knowledge of the context, including experience of a particular sport at a certain level and of performing at the same venues, will help.

The head coach of a women's football team described to me some of the impression cues that she picked up on while watching academy games and how important this aspect of leadership is: "I know the younger players, and our under-15s were playing in the cup final. I came with my lawyer friend, and we sat in the directors' box. She has a good base knowledge of the sport, but when I was sitting next to her, I was watching everything. I would say to her, 'Do you think he's tired or does it look like he doesn't care?' She said, 'No, I think he looks unfit.' That gave me a good insight about her depth of understanding. She was watching the game, but I was watching what's underneath that game, what the coach was doing, how players were reacting to criticism, and that's the fascinating thing. It's not about tactic or technique; it's about everything beneath that. I know some really good technical coaches, but they might as well talk to a log."

Leaders capable of reading the moods of team members can work with them to channel those moods into more effective behaviour.[7] Modifying behaviour is part of leadership, but only an empathic leader understands the starting point. This work requires you to consider how an individual or team will behave in each situation and what can be done to improve that behaviour. In effect, this pre-empts unwanted behaviour. A men's football head coach explained to me that by gaining an understanding of how a player was likely to behave, he is able to improve their performance: "In this group, I have a guy who is never resting, he is like on fire all the time, he is like a wind that blows in. We were playing a diamond formation and he is a full-back. This means he has to decide when to go to intercept the ball played to the winger or when to back off. So the main thing is to be calm and make good decisions. I knew this guy would go all the time, every time. This causes problems. He did this in a game; my prediction was right. We had a mental coach speak to him about this . . . and I explained it to him, and we continue to work on him and with him."

Knowing how a player is likely to react in an imagined situation was described by an international volleyball head coach as "invaluable knowledge", The knowledge has to be accurate, and it is the same for recognising potential.

Recognising Potential

An understanding of the inner world and behaviours of team members helps a leader to predict the potential of each individual. Empathic leaders in elite sport sometimes surprise fans or the media with the decisions they make. Often this is due to the head coach knowing significantly more about his athletes and better understanding the contexts they are asked to perform in. A men's football head coach explained to me how confident he was about introducing a young player into his team, based on what he knew about him: "In our club, this winter, we needed centre backs and contacted two experienced centre backs. But they weren't able to come at the time, and then they were not ready to play games, so we put a 19-year-old in who might not have thought he'd get game time. It's been a roller coaster, but very good, and people are forgetting his age and lack of experience during the ups and downs. If you don't see things from his point of view, you'd determine him to not be good enough or ready. I've been working closely with the boy and giving him a lot of feedback from game to game, and it's interesting to see how much better he became in five games, with such a jump in level."

Recognising the potential of athletes can be a major factor in determining the success of a coach, particularly if the individual introduced soon becomes their best performer. Another men's football head coach told me the following story: "My best player last year was a boy who had some problems, some issues, all the talent in the world, but he never seemed to show all his talent in a game or even in training. You could never get the best out of him. So he became a kind of project for me. Eventually, we struck up a really close relationship. In the two years he played with me, he scored the most goals he'd ever scored, got the most assists, and was the best player not just in our team but in the whole league. I think that was due to me taking time to understand him, to get to know him, to understand about his childhood. You know, he told me about his problems and his issues, and we ended up having an open dialogue. And when he wasn't performing, I could come down on him and be truthful with him. I learned what to look out for. I could be hard on him, but also give him a pat on the back when he needed it. Me, understanding him and what he was capable of gave me an opportunity to be able to do that. It's funny, when I left the club, the staff called me and asked, 'How did you handle him? We can't deal with him.' They always used to say to me, 'God, why do you spend so much time with him?' It was because, as a coach, I had to recognise when someone was going to become pivotal to my team. He still calls me now. He's just signed a contract in another country. He called me yesterday and asked for advice and asked how I was doing. That shows the relationship we had."

When it comes to recognising potential, it is not always about the potential to perform well at the sport. Despite an athlete having talent, a cricket head coach told me that other factors can restrict their potential: "We had a player. Unbelievable talent, but he was an absolutely shit bloke. And he played for us, did really well, got picked for the national team. We were like, 'This will be interesting.' Then his national team are on the phone, saying, 'This bloke's great, we want him back in and in the test team.' I was like, 'What?' They said, 'Yeah, in the test team by the summer.' I put the phone down and thought, 'Are we talking about the same fucking person?' Six months later, the head coach of the national team calls and says, 'This bloke will never play for us again.' He couldn't sustain his behaviours. He'd gone in, played a role, brilliant team man and all that, but he couldn't sustain it. When he was under pressure, his true colours came out and then they got rid of him."

Retaining the right talent is a challenge for leaders, and one not necessarily based on ability. A handball head coach told me about a difficult decision he had to make. He said this concerned "one of the most talented athletes we ever had. He was constantly distracted by things in his personal life. We tried to help him, but just couldn't get anywhere. He didn't want things to change. So we moved him on and, despite his talent, he's never done anything in the game, which is sad, but as far as this club goes, we got that right."

Situations and Reactions

Empathic leaders use their understanding of the personal attributes of team members to predict how they will perform in a certain role, while remaining aware of what their limitations are. An international rugby union head coach told me, "If we know someone who isn't right for a role and hasn't the personality, I'll get another player in. A more suitable personality. So if *John Doe* is an outstanding talent and a leader on the pitch, but not off, if he hates being in meetings, he'll train hard and play hard, but getting him into a meeting is only ticking a box – it won't achieve anything – so I don't ask him unless I have to. That's just knowing your players. It's not that his personality is wrong; it's just how he is driven. Would I go to war with him? Yes, but I wouldn't go to a meeting with him."

It will become apparent to an empathic leader that certain team members are better in certain situations, or moments, including high-pressure scenarios. An international handball head coach told me, "I have a very technically gifted player who cannot cope under pressure. So, if a match is tight, I might bring him off, and bring on someone with less technical ability, who's less exciting to watch but more reliable in that situation. That's about learning and understanding the character of the player. You have to try and have the right players on court for the moment. It's about knowing who wants and can handle the responsibility required of the moment."

The head coach of a women's football team told me, "If you go into a cup final, you need to know how each of them will emotionally cope and perform. Sometimes you need to balance that out. For one particular final, the best player we had was emotionally driven and wouldn't have coped, but, I thought, if they are the best player, how do I manage that? Do you play them or are they a risk – they might get sent-off. It's going to be really competitive. What's best for the team? It wasn't an easy one."

The context of these decisions is also taken into consideration too. Variables like the venue, crowd and atmosphere, and the current team climate will impact on behaviours. A female head coach of a women's football team provided the following example: "The fans here can be really horrible at times and at first it used to really bother me. I wanted to ask: if they had a daughter, would they want someone to treat them like that? A club this size, you need to understand where these people are coming from, but it's very difficult. It's brutal here. It can be 90 minutes of spewing hatred. They support the team, but how can you prepare players for that environment? You can't replicate that in training, where they might be performing well. Fifty thousand fans might be telling them they're shit, after one bad touch."

Empathic leaders feel their way into contexts to gain understanding and to appreciate the impact they have on their team. The head coach of a football team in North America told me, "You consider which players will handle certain scenarios, certain atmospheres, and which players are going to struggle. It's also part of your preparation in the week leading up to the game. Depending on the stadium, the atmosphere you're going to play in, that becomes part of your preparation, part of your tactics almost."

An international football head coach explained how he prepares his team when playing in a certain Central American capital city, where he recognises the atmosphere influences both teams: "Going into a city that's the murder capital of the world, it's a world unto itself. The home team are beasts when they are there in front of and with their people; when they play away, they don't have the same thing going on, they are more uncomfortable. And our players going into that atmosphere – you can tell the ones that have an appetite for it and the ones that don't want to be there. The ones who just don't deal with it. In the build-up, you can see, a week out, that they are getting nervous of the atmosphere or the heat. You can only try to explain that we've done everything we can for them to prepare."

At elite level in sport, details matter. As another football head coach told me, "The more you understand someone, the better perspective you have on how they will react in certain scenarios. Today, at this ground, with that crowd, are they going to stay with their man on a set piece, little details like that? Are they going to track their runner from midfield? Are they going to accept responsibility when they've made a mistake? The more you understand and know someone, the better chance you have of knowing all of this and getting the best out of them."

In football, one of the highest-pressure situations for athletes to deal with is taking a penalty kick. Just 12 yards out and with only the goalkeeper to beat, they are expected to score. No matter how talented the footballer is, the pressure of the situation can change everything. Empathic leaders of teams in elite sport don't just know their athletes, but they also understand how they are thinking and feeling in such situations.

The head coach of a women's football team told me, "I had a big player of ours last year telling me she wanted to take one. I went with that, and she missed. But I would choose her again if she wanted one. It just didn't go right for her in that moment. I loved taking penalties as a player, I always felt I'd score. I was always positive. Other players I know, go, 'This ain't for me.'" The head coach then reminded me that there are a number of other details that can induce even more pressure. In the following example from the same head coach, one of his athletes knew an opponent well enough to empathise accurately and predict what she was thinking: "We had one at the weekend, one of the players had to take a pen against her ex-keeper. She'd played with her for two years and so they'll know what to expect from each other, so there's a greater emotion to the situation. There's more understanding there. More pressure on the taker, maybe, because she knows how good the keeper is. But I know what she knows, and she scored a great penalty. It was a different type of penalty to one I've seen her take before because she was aware of the keeper's perspective. And it worked, so, you know, I think it's really key to understand the players."

When an empathic leader understands that pressure situations impact on certain athletes, they can take action to remedy the situation. An Australian head coach told me, "We had one guy, he couldn't handle big games. I could see it in him days beforehand. We got him to work with our psychologist and now he's a different bloke." The head coach was able to update what he knew of this player, and now he considers the player more often in the kind of games and situations that the player once found challenging.

The pressures felt by athletes begin at youth level. Sometimes this is when a head coach first notices how pressure affects them. A cricket head coach described observing youth players training one day. He noticed that boys who were practising were suddenly taking fewer risks. He looked around and realised that this coincided with the boys' parents entering the viewing gallery. The head coach understood how this was making the boys feel and why it had altered their behaviour. He took immediate action, changing the way things were done: "That's when I banned all the parents," he said. "Because of their behaviour changes. You want them to have fun like kids in a park just playing, and that's one of the barriers." This change in the context – specifically, who was watching them – had completely changed the experience these players were enjoying. Once this added pressure was removed, the boys began taking risks once again.

Another head coach warned that no matter how empathic you are and how well you know the athletes, you never really know how an athlete will respond until you have seen them in the same situation: "I had a player I dropped to change a team shape, and she was very professional, and I knew her well, but I didn't really know for certain how she'd react, and I wondered, you know, because until you've seen someone in that situation, no matter how well you know them, you never know how they'll react. Thankfully, she was fine. And she came on and did well. It could have easily gone the other way. I've had that surprise, where I've thought, 'I didn't see that coming.'"

Being dropped from the team will create very different responses depending on the individual. Pre-empting this reaction with mentalising to try to understand the most likely reaction will help a leader to decide how to convey the news. Empathic leaders understand how information will be received because they understand the inner world of the receiver. It's something that is important to get right, because the reactions of one athlete can have negative repercussions for the whole team.

The timing of informing an athlete they have been dropped can make all the difference. The head coach of a women's international football team offered me his thoughts on this: "It would be silly of me as the manager to tell a player they were dropped just before kick-off. I mean, that would be crushing, finding out you've been cut at that moment." I asked other head coaches about this. An ice hockey head coach also expressed concerns about negative reactions and how they can impact the rest of the team. He told me, "I do it the day before a game. If you tell them the day of the game, their reaction could impact the rest of the players. If it's the day before, their impact won't affect the players on game day. And I don't think the individual player needs to prepare the night before the game, emotionally and physically, to be told just before that they are not playing. That will make their reaction worse too."

Dropping an athlete will never be easy or come without negative implications. It can be more difficult when the athlete is an established star. Head coaches can plan their action using the knowledge they have accrued and by imagining reactions.[5] Situations such as this provide an opportunity to demonstrate empathic leadership, and to do so will add to a leader's reputation, which will have positive consequences for relationships.

Although knowing the athletes well is the goal, head coaches are likely to draw on relevant experiences of their own too to inform their predictions about reactions to novel situations. A male head coach of a women's football team described a situation that he had no previous experience of: "There have been games when I've found out halfway through that they are playing against their ex-girlfriend! That's never happened to me. I couldn't imagine playing against my ex-girlfriends. So that emotional state is something you've got to think about, because how is that going to go?"

A leader will never be able to know everything about their team members, but empathic leaders make constant efforts to learn. A head coach of a men's football team described to me how it works for him: "You put yourself in the position of the player and get to know his background a little bit, and that's more difficult now that you get players from all around the world. This is something for anyone coming into contact with a new culture, not just in sport. When I first became a coach, I had some experiences with African players, and to be honest I didn't even reflect on it. But then after a while in the job, I started to scout players in Africa and meet people in the Middle East, and your knowledge grows. You get a better perspective and know more about different players, and then it makes it easier to understand people from those places and to predict how they might act in different situations."

Understanding Rivals

An empathic leader can predict the actions of leaders or team members representing rival teams or organisations.[6] As former England cricket captain, now psychoanalyst, Mike Brearley says, "leadership is about knowing how your people tick and knowing how the opposition tick".[8] It is more difficult when your rival is a stranger. As reflected in the famous instruction (often attributed to Sun Tzu) to keep your friends close and your enemies closer, by knowing the rival a leader has an advantage.[9] It enables a leader to accurately predict the behaviour of whoever they are up against. The more you know a rival, the more accurately you will be able to empathise and, therefore, the more advantage you can gain. As an international rugby union head coach explained to me, "If you coach against your ex-players, you know what makes them tick." Understanding what makes the opposition tick is an important part of being an empathic leader in elite sport.[8] It will also help you to empower your team and individual athletes with knowledge that can make a difference.

There are many variables related to leadership strategy and performance, but success often requires an understanding of the motives, feelings, and likely behaviours of rivals.[10] Employing emotional empathy to achieve this can be draining, and an empathic leader will be experiencing enough vicarious emotions already. For interactions with rivals, leaders will be better off using cognitive empathy – mentalising – rather than experiencing the emotions of the other. This provides the knowledge required to understand rivals' emotional states and perspectives without feeling them. By focusing on cognitive empathic processes rather than emotional, an empathic leader is being self-protective.[11]

Knowledge gained through experience can also be applied to predict the behaviour of opponents. Head coaches can understand the perspectives and intentions of other athletes and coaches more accurately if they have experienced the same situation. This was illustrated by what an ice hockey head coach told me about taking the opponent's perspective, although he had not realised that this was being empathic. He said, "You try and look at it from their perspective. I'm not sure it's empathising, but you definitely do that. I know that if the other coach is struggling to win a game and he's playing in front of his own fans, he will feel under a lot of pressure, and that will impact on his selection and tactics. I know how he is feeling and what he is thinking, so I guess it is empathy after all."

Perspective taking is empathic behaviour, and all of the head coaches I've spoken to do this. An international rugby union head coach told me, "You do look at their last performance and put yourself in the opposition manager's shoes, and you think how he will be feeling and thinking. That's absolutely something we do. We always have a proportion of focus on what the opposition are thinking, and we do put ourselves in their shoes, so in that respect we are using empathy."

The reason that these coaches paused to consider whether or not what they are doing is an empathic skill is no doubt because empathy is more typically associated with pro-social behaviour or compassion. You need to remember that empathy is about understanding and gathering knowledge; what you do with that understanding is up to you. An international volley-ball head coach said to me, "I often put myself in their position in order to gain an understanding of their intentions, and then I react to that know-ledge by playing my players a certain way or selecting certain players in cer-tain positions. I also observe the way the other team is in the warm-up. If maybe I see something there, an injury or something, then I imagine what would make that situation worse for them, and try and get my players to do that somehow. Sometimes I see them using dark arts, whether that's time wasting, breaking up a rhythm of a game. I can gauge that by seeing it from their point of view. I can tell why they are doing that. It's all knowledge."

For the team to be successful, leaders have to encourage high levels of empathic accuracy in their team members. In elite sport, athletes who under-stand the intentions and motivations of rival athletes will be at an advan-tage. For athletes to understand the opposition's approach, a head coach can attempt to mimic it in training. The head coach of a netball team told me, "We set up scenarios where we get players in training to act like the opposition, and there are always players we can get to do that." A rugby union head coach said, "We get our younger teams to play like the opposition and that kind of thing." These practices supply players with greater understanding and knowledge. Facing an imitation of how the opposition will play, will improve athletes' predictions and reactions during competition. However, sometimes knowledge can be gained from the specific body language of rival athletes, which will be unique to each individual. The emotional cli-mate of rival teams will also be unique to them.

Observing the body language and emotional climate of opponents is part of the work of an empathic leader. A women's football head coach said to me, "I look at the body language of other teams, how they react to goals and things and what we feel we can do. If we score early, how will they react to that and what will they do." Some head coaches admitted to me that they go further still.

An international football head coach told me, "When I coached with another coach, when we played in the World Cup, we had a whiteboard at the side of the pitch, and we had a photograph of the opposition's starting eleven. So he pinned this on our whiteboard so that the opposition bench could see it. That seemed to worry them. He did a lot of things like that because he knew what would unsettle them. He saw it from their perspective."

Experience, together with the time and effort a leader is willing to put into relationships will determine how empathically accurate they become. An international hockey head coach said to me, "I have a better understanding of the players' perspectives, by putting in the time to get to know them on different levels, and that negates the draining aspect because I'm more likely to do things right. I'm not left wondering how they are going to react when I see them next. I know."

Armed with information, a head coach can make more informed decisions. This may help to resolve dilemmas over selection or other decisions that have to be made in the build-up to competition or during a game. It can also help to undermine the intentions of rivals. In summary, the empathic leader has greater knowledge, and so can better predict behaviour, reactions, performances, and potential, which means they have a distinct advantage.

Notes

1. Ickes, W. J. (1997). *Empathic accuracy*. Guilford Press.
2. Goleman, D. & Boyatzis, R. (2008). Social intelligence and the biology of leadership. *Harvard Business Review*, 86(9), 74–81.
3. Schneider, R. C. (2013). Emotional intelligence: The overlooked component of sport leadership. *International Journal of Sport and Society*, 3(3), 43–56.
4. Khosravi, B. G., Manafi, M., Hojabri, R., Farhadi, F. & Ghesmi, R. (2011). The impact of emotional intelligence towards the effectiveness of delegation: A study in banking industry in Malaysia. *International Journal of Business and Social Science*, 2(18), 93–99.

5. Lorimer, R. (2013). The development of empathic accuracy in sports coaches. *Journal of Sport Psychology in Action*, 4(1), 26–33.

6. Lorimer, R. & Jowett, S. (2009). Empathic accuracy in coach–athlete dyads who participate in team and individual sports. *Psychology of Sport and Exercise*, 10(1), 152–158.

7. O'Neil, D. A. (2011). The value of emotional intelligence for high performance coaching: A commentary. *International Journal of Sports Science and Coaching*, 6(3), 315–328.

8. Brearley, M. (2013). CSCLeaders Talks 2013 – Mike Brearley, former England Cricket captain, on leadership (PwC, London). Vimeo. https://vimeo.com/62854436

9. Zaki, J. (2014). Empathy: A motivated account. *Psychological Bulletin*, 140(6), 1608–1647. doi:10.1037/a0037679

10. Galinsky, A. D., Maddux, W. W., Gilin, D. & White, J. B. (2008). Why it pays to get inside the head of your opponent: The differential effects of perspective taking and empathy in negotiations. *Psychological Science*, 19(4), 378–384.

11. Mackes, N. K., Golm, D., O'Daly, O. G., Sarkar, S., Sonuga-Barke, E. J. S., Fairchild, G. & Mehta, M. A. (2018). Tracking emotions in the brain – Revisiting the Empathic Accuracy Task. *Neuroimage*, 178, 677–686.

Developing Empathy　　　　　　　　**7**

More and more organisations are turning to empathic leadership, but the focus of this is often limited to relationships between leaders and team members. This ignores the fact that leaders are responsible for the climate of the team or organisation they lead. The contagious nature of empathy means that empathic leaders will affect intra-team or intra-organisation relationships. However, empathic leaders are tasked with going further. Actively encouraging empathy in others is understood to be part of an empathic leader's broader responsibilities.[1,2] There is a good reason for this. Research has shown that empathy inspires cohesion in social groups, and this has positive consequences for team performance.[3,4] Many of the highest performing business organisations are now working hard to develop empathy, not just in their leaders but in all of their employees.[5] Yet for teams of athletes in elite sport, such efforts are at the discretion of the head coach. This presents another opportunity for empathic leaders in elite sport to gain an advantage over those leaders who fail to value empathy.

Developing empathy must begin with leadership. The example of empathy is often said to be the best way of encouraging empathy in a group.[1,6] It would be no good developing empathy within a team and then installing an outdated, autocratic leader. Such leaders need not give up. Research has shown that developing empathy is possible in almost everyone, even narcissists.[7] Other than specific training, there are a number of ways that you can develop empathy. There is evidence showing that mindfulness and meditation enhance empathy.[8–10] Neuroscientists have confirmed that meditative practices increase the grey matter of the *angular gyrus*, a region of the brain that is associated with empathy.[11]

DOI: 10.4324/9781003324676-8

Other ways of developing empathy include reading fiction,[12] visiting the theatre,[13] or cinema,[14] watching television dramas,[15] acting, and creative writing.[16] These activities require you to become fictional characters in order to understand perspectives. Sometimes you'll do this cognitively and other times you will be feeling with the characters. Either way, this is literally practising empathy. As you get to know characters, you will find you are better at predicting their behaviour and more understanding of their intentions and motivations. The fact that these characters are fictional does not matter;[17] you are learning to see the world from another's perspective. If you attempt to act, you have to become the other in an even deeper way. You will have to consider your body language, your history and experiences, and how you interact with other characters. As a writer, you need to be able to see through the eyes of all of your characters at all times, maintaining multiple perspectives. Few jobs require empathy more than being a fiction writer.

Empathy also develops through life experiences.[18] Empathy begins after we leave the womb. We are born with a capacity for empathy, not with empathy.[19] Our unique life experiences and social learning decide how our personal development of empathy proceeds.[19, 20] The environment we experience begins with the one provided by our parents and widens with the relationships and culture we are surrounded by.[21] Therefore, a leader's life experience, even before their career has begun, is likely to have a substantial influence on their leadership style, and their emotional response to a situation is unconsciously connected to their history.[22] You will always find it easier to empathise with someone going through a situation that you have been through yourself. Experience has long been a desired leadership quality, and empathic leaders can utilise their experiences in their relationships with others.

A cricket head coach explained to me why he feels that his own experiences helped him to become a more empathic leader: "I wasn't much good as a player, and I had a lot of injuries. I had moments where I showed glimpses of ability and talent, but I had quite a long career without being hugely successful, and I had lots of setbacks. As a result of that, I understand quite a myriad of experiences within the game. So I've had some success, but not consistent success like a lot of people. I've experienced second-team cricket, I've experienced first-team cricket, I've experienced being dropped, poor coaches, good coaches; all incredibly valuable experiences, and you don't realise their value at the time." I asked this head coach if there were experiences he lacked that he would appreciate having in his memory bank now. He said, "I haven't played international cricket. I played first-class cricket, but if I were to be an international head coach, I wonder, can I be empathic to people in that environment?"

A women's football head coach also expressed to me her concerns that she lacked the experience of playing at the highest level. She said, "I've often asked myself if I lack empathy due to my lack of experience." This is not necessarily the case. Anyone can become an empathic leader. Experience is helpful but not mandatory. Perspective taking or mentalising can offer a leader insight of an experience they may not have encountered in their own life.

A handball head coach offered me his thoughts on this: "I've played under some great coaches who haven't played so much; I think there's always going to be players who think, 'Yeah, but you haven't really done it, have you? So you don't understand my world.' As unfair as that may be, it's always there. You can still have empathy for people. But I do refer to my experiences if I think it will help. We played away recently, and we were getting beaten heavily, and I can say, 'Look, I've been here a hell of a lot more times than you have, and I'm still here. The scoreboard might not look great, but it's okay. These are the things that you need to consider, these are the things that will happen, and this is what you need to do.' This comes from a position of understanding. They see I'm not criticising them for it, that I've experienced it a bunch of times, and that I know what they are feeling and have to do."

An international football head coach told me that he knew he had the relevant expereince but worried that his empathic skills were lacking. Empathy became a focus for him as soon as he realised its benefits. He said, "In the past, I'd been accused of not having any empathy. Maybe, because of that, I worked on it for the last few years, and I've realised the positive effect you can have on people if you understand them. In the past, I had a negative impact on players early on and I hated that, it was like I was the coach that I'd had, and I knew I needed to put that right. It made me feel awful. I've gone away and thought about it, and now I believe that I pass empathy on to others."

Empathy can be passed on to team members, as explained by another football head coach: "I think how empathic I am as a coach translates to the players. I think, you know, my personality, my empathy, that definitely rubs off on them. It's not a conscious thing; it just happens."

Developing Empathy in Teams

Once an empathic leader is in place, the empathy within the group can become a priority. Research has shown that where empathy is developed, team spirit and job satisfaction will improve.[23] There is evidence showing that empathy training programmes can be successful,[24] and as a consequence there has been a dramatic increase in empathy training across industries throughout the world.

There are now a number of school programmes including *Roots of Empathy*,[25] which began in Canada, and *Step By Step*,[26] in Denmark. In medicine, there are empathy programmes too, to help medical teams and individual medics develop more empathy for each other and their patients, since empathy has been found to speed up healing time.[27–30] This is also relevant to the treatment of athletes in elite sport. Whether you are the head coach, a member of the medical staff, or a teammate, empathising with injured athletes will help get them back to fitness faster.

Business schools around the world are also providing empathy programmes for their students.[5] In 2018, the world's first empathy training for diplomats began.[31] The Center for Empathy in International Affairs (CEIA) aims to enhance the empathy skills of international officials, diplomats, mediators, and practitioners, in order for them to gain a deeper understanding of others and use this understanding in their work. Organisations across industries now employ psychologists and empathy trainers to help develop empathy.[32] Whatever the industry, if the work involves people and relationships, developing empathy will prove beneficial.

Empathy helps to create a shared existence for a team. It is the bridge that connects people.[33] The traditional approach to developing empathy in groups is through the training of communication skills, such as dialogue,[34, 35] and active listening.[36] Empathy can also be developed by using perspective-taking or role-taking instructions,[37] but making these behaviours habitual will take time.[38] The right approach will be different for each team depending on the context and the individuals involved.

Athletes in elite sport arrive at clubs at various stages of life, with different degrees of empathic ability. With athletes coming from a variety of countries and cultures, achieving team cohesion can be a problem for leaders. There are various approaches to developing empathy in teams in elite sport that are being employed already. To begin with, athletes need to gain understanding of the lives and backgrounds of their teammates. Sharing biographical stories and listening to experiences of others softens boundaries and sows the seeds of empathy and connection.[39] Work like this encourages a listening culture in the group. It not only shares knowledge of each other but also engages athletes in the act of listening to stories, providing an opportunity to practise empathy.[12]

Biographical stories ask the listener to take the perspective of the protagonist. As well as listening to teammates, it can be useful for leaders and athletes to read biographies. Domain-specific life stories are likely to be more useful, and so reading biographies of people in sport can prove to be effective empathy training. However, learning about the people you are working with is more valuable.

A hockey head coach described one of his practices to me: "I get them all to do a five-minute presentation. To get them to talk on themselves, what's import to them in their lives, and it can be very moving at times. Maybe a big event has happened in someone's past that you weren't aware of. Again, if we are talking about empathy, you know they approach a situation in a certain way . . . their lens or perspective on certain things. It gives me that understanding of why someone is behaving the way they are, and it informs their teammates similarly. But I can have more empathy when I have discussions with them, which hopefully means the outcomes are going to be more positive, whether that's on them personally or on them as a player. It's formal, but more informal. We are not directly talking about sport. I'd probably argue that the other stuff is more important to gain a more in-depth understanding of a person. And knowing how they might tend to react when I talk to them during a game is important."

An ice hockey head coach told me about a session he ran: "I asked the whole squad to meet me after lunch in our meeting room and to bring a story of a moment in which they first realised this was going to be their profession. I was worried nobody would say anything, but, wow, did we listen to some great stories that day."

A football head coach told me that, in his experience, "stories create connections". I asked him how he sets out his sessions. He said, "We've called it Heroes, Hardships and Highlights. So they tell the rest of us about their heroes in the game, hardships they've been through, and their highlights, and I gave the first one, to show them the way. They could present a PowerPoint if they wanted to, and they could speak about whatever they wanted to. That was it. Some of them just put up a picture of David Beckham, saying, 'Cos I like his free kicks, he was a hero of mine. Hardships was an injury I had last year. My highlight was when I won the title when I was an under-15.' But some of them spoke about losing parents in front of a whole new group, and I'm choking, and I really feel it. You see that people have decided to lay it out, and some actually put up a picture of a parent they lost. And that was what I wanted to do, to try to create a culture of everyone understanding each other. And what that person has been through, others may have. Everything resonates with at least someone in the group, and it forms connections."

A handball head coach described running similar sessions with his athletes, but also getting them out of the context and into alternative spaces, which he finds reveals more about them. He said, "When you get

teams made up of people from different cultures and countries, it's a great
thing to get them to tell each other about where they come from and swap
stories – it's a really great thing to do. But I like to put them in situations
away from sport to help them understand what their skills are, you know,
what they do with their free time, other interests . . . The more I know
about a player, the better I can connect with them, and the more they know
about each other, the better they connect with each other as well." I asked
him what kind of things he has discovered about his athletes by doing this:
"Oh, loads of things, yeah. Lots of musicians, impressionists, actors, or
things like that. It's fascinating – they have all these different skills, and
you'd never guess. One was a film critic . . . he reviewed films, and I'm into
films, so there's a personal bond now there."

Earlier in this book, I explored hugging as a symbol of the close
relationships between head coaches and their team members. Physical contact between team members helps to communicate empathy, too.[40] Our
skin is a social organ.[41] Research shows that a release of the hormone oxytocin, something known to enhance in-group cooperation, is a consequence
of empathic behaviour such as social touch.[42] Although being in a close relationship in itself has a positive impact on emotions, this is enhanced with
physical contact.[43] Social touch has been shown to increase behavioural synchrony,[44] and it conveys resonance and support to others.[45]

Moving together can also play a role. Studies of ballet dancers have
shown a relationship between empathy and moving in synchrony.[46]
Synchrony, cohesion, and resonance are all sought by leaders of teams.
The benefits in sport are regularly documented, and there is evidence in
sporting history too.

In 1967, Celtic Football Club upset the odds to become the first British
team to win the European Cup. All but two of the 15-man squad were born
within ten miles of their ground in Glasgow, Scotland. They came through
the youth teams together and knew each other inside out. This must have
been significant in them managing to come from behind to defeat the
much-favoured Italian team, Inter Milan, 2–1. As Celtic's club website says
today, those local players formed "a cohesive and interrelated team unit
that ploughed a path through Europe". That season, Celtic also won the
Scottish League, Scottish Cup, Scottish League Cup, and the Glasgow Cup,
and the team were declared to be the greatest club football side of all time
in the world by a recent BBC poll.[47] There are numerous other examples of
groups of athletes outperforming expectation due to the cohesion of the
group. The power of team cohesion should not be underestimated.

A handball head coach told me, "The group I have at present, a lot
of them went to school together and that helps. When you get teams

made up of people from different cultures and countries, it's a great thing to get them to tell each other about where they come from and swap stories – it's a really great thing to do. It makes a group aligned and brings cohesion."

Head coaches working today do everything they can to create cohesion because they know how important it is to performance. A rugby union head coach I spoke with told me that he likes to include the families of athletes in this, which enables an even deeper understanding of one another. He said, "We run a crèche that's very popular; it's massively used. We have coffee mornings each week for the wives as none are from this area, so it's important they have a meeting place. The wives also have two gym sessions a week; that's run by the interns – it's good for the wives and the interns. All sorts of things are put in place to make the families comfortable and connected." The closer families and athletes become, the greater the cohesion, and the more empathic they will be towards each other.

An international football head coach told me, "Family too is huge – to get an understanding of their family dynamic. We have group socials where families meet each other, and it helps understand one another a bit better." Another head coach told me that he is always focused on getting families in the environment, stating: "By knowing each other well, we understand each other better and become a more cohesive group and team." Head coaches have also described encouraging family members to attend games and spend time with the families of other elite athletes.

When empathy spreads through groups, the resultant behaviours will tend to be prosocial and altruistic.[2] Understanding of another person's family situation will often explain their behaviour. A cricket head coach told me, "We have one player, currently a consistent performer, as soon as the day's finished, he's gone. The others are like, 'He doesn't stay for a drink, he's miserable.' I'm like, 'No, no, you need to understand. He has family, two young kids, he's this kind of personality, he needs time away. If he spends all his time with you guys, he's fucked. He needs to get his energy back.' So you have to create that understanding. The players are very judgemental. It's a lack of awareness, so that's what we do. We're constantly trying to get people to gain a wider understanding of themselves and the other players in the environment. If someone wants to go for a few beers, that's okay too, you know. This is not school. But it's what you need to do, and without being judgemental of others. And not to drag people with you. It won't work."

A rugby union head coach said, "When some of the players have built closer relationships between their families, that brings the group tighter together. There's a greater understanding of each other as a result. The closer they get, the easier they can predict how other players are feeling or thinking, so, ultimately, we are encouraging empathy."

One of the advantages of building empathy and cohesion within a group is that it leads to greater resilience. An international lacrosse head coach said: "I think that's important on the field of play . . . We had resilience as a team because what you've done by building those bonds by a more emotional intelligence approach, a more empathic approach between the players, you have trust and respect, and when the proverbial hits the fan, Dave's got my back, Ian's going to come through."

In the context of elite sport, leaders are often dealing with regular changes of personnel as athletes move between clubs, and head coaches come and go too. As a women's football head coach told me, this can inhibit team cohesion: "If there are changes, you have to try to retain that team cohesion. Knowing athletes over a longer period is more advantageous. The longer a group is together, the more they know about each other, and then they can just give a look that means a hundred words."

When a head coach is familiar with a group, it can be used to their advantage. A cricket head coach explained his situation to me: "This sounds really wrong, or arrogant, but I'm the perfect fit for this club right now. Most of the guys I had in the academy, I identified, and I brought them into the team. I have a nucleus of players who have absolute faith and trust in me. My captain, for example, I've known for a long time; our philosophies are aligned. If the club went to him today and said right, we are getting rid of the head coach, he'd say, 'No, no way, if you do that, I'm going.' That's how strongly he feels about the relationship. And that's putting words in his mouth, but it's how I think it is, and I am the right fit for right now."

Any practising of empathic skills will help team members to understand other people better. An international lacrosse head coach told me that he has been creative about the ways in which he can get his athletes thinking about the lives of others. He said, "I got a game over Christmas called *Sussed* and I'll play that with players. It's who in your group would you most like to have on your side in a zombie apocalypse? Who in the team would eat the last doughnut? It's about doing it in a fun and safe environment, where they are sharing thoughts and ideas and understanding each other as people."

Head coaches have described other games that they have used to develop empathy across a group. One head coach told me about how he sows the seeds of conversations with cubes. He said, "We maximise any time we have together; we have *conversation* cubes, like six-year-olds use. We develop our own conversation cubes, and they'll sit in groups of six or seven and roll the dice, and wherever it lands, there's a question or something, and they start to discover more about each other. Like, what's your biggest fear? All we insist is that people listen; they don't have to tell their own stories, but they have to listen to what others say. There are all sorts of small things you can do to get to know your teammates better."

Getting athletes to share personal thoughts and philosophies is part of the process of encouraging empathy. Whenever they are together, it provides an opportunity to increase interpersonal understanding. This includes being on tour or playing away games. An international lacrosse head coach told me, "I'd like to think we also develop empathy in the squad a bit more implicitly as well, where we might manipulate rooming lists where we put particular people together. We might manipulate who feeds back on game play after a training session . . . At the last World Championships, we let the players come up with a list of one, two, three, who they'd want to room with. On previous tours, we always said, 'No, we are telling you who you are going with.' At that stage, we were manipulating by putting an experienced player with a less experienced player; maybe it's matching up sleep pattern or whatever else. But for the actual World Championships, we said, 'Look, we want you to reflect on all of those experiences and reflect on that and decide who you want to room with, but move away from the "Jo's my mate so I want to room with Jo". It's okay, I've got a better understanding of who I'm compatible with, who has the same sleep patterns, who throws their socks on the floor where I like to be tidy.' Getting them to just understand more about each other as people and take for read that that means they know more about each other as players. So it's both explicit and implicit too."

An international football head coach described some of the social events he has organised in order to get his athletes to reveal more about themselves. He said, "I had a player who, after a music festival we attended, we discovered he was an amazing musician, and nobody knew! We realised because of that we knew he had a different cerebral capacity and potential, and all the other players appreciated that about him. It also allows his teammates a back door in when I want to communicate with him, if that makes sense. They can mention the music as a way to initiate a chat, now they know that's his thing." Such knowledge can determine whether or not conversations happen, and that influences relationships.

The understanding that is developed between athletes includes knowledge of the limits of their emotions. This is different for each person and influenced by life experiences. A women's football head coach said that the sharing of stories had helped his team with this. He said, "It was great to see people open up and talk about things, and it also helped me when I'm saying things and how I say them. You know, humour and banter and stuff in football is a real tough subject. It is rife and it's something you do in the workplace, but if you don't know the person that you're saying a joke to, or what they've been through, then offence can be taken even if it's not meant to be given. Until I know a person, I don't know what they've been through. Understanding them was really key."

Emotional responses to a situation can be consciously or unconsciously connected to an athlete's history,[22] and knowledge of this is likely to be dependent on the length of time the athletes have been together and the kind of relationships they have. The more that group members know of this history, the more appropriate care they can take.

Head coaches and athletes are able to see and feel other perspectives through time spent together. By understanding each other, athletes can work effectively with cohesion and resilience towards common goals.[48] These variables can be enhanced via the development of empathy, and they will be valuable to any team seeking success.[4]

The Roles of Others

Empathy development can be achieved in training-ground situations by asking athletes to understand the roles of others. A netball head coach told me that she insists that her athletes have an empathic approach to their work, and that they are constantly considering other perspectives, particularly those of their teammates. Concerning one athlete, she said, "I had to get her to see that it's a team game. 'People are trying,' I've said to her. 'You've got to see their perspective.' She needs to know that she's not the only one on the court. I also added that if she doesn't have empathy for her teammates and what they're trying to help her with, then she will not be on the court."

Developing a greater understanding of the perspectives of teammates can be helped by training sessions focusing on role rotation of athletes. A rugby union head coach described his training sessions: "Sometimes we rotate roles on the pitch, so that the players get an idea of what it's like for someone else. They learn that if so-and-so is here, he won't want the ball played to him like that; he'll want it like this."

It is also important for team members to understand the perspectives of their opponents. If they can understand their opponent's intentions and predict their actions, they can limit their impact in competition. This can be improved through watching the opponents in action as much as possible, with the aim of getting to a point where their behaviour becomes predictable.

Developing empathy within an elite team must begin with the leader of that team. Empathy can spread through a team due to its contagious nature and will be helped along by specific practices designed to develop empathy within the team. Empathy allows athletes to become psychologically in tune with others. It encourages cohesion, resilience, alignment, better communication, and a more caring climate. This was summed up by another head coach, who said: "Ultimately, sharing stories and experiences will help foster empathy and team harmony. And that's what we want."

Notes

1. Tzouramani, E. (2017). Leadership and empathy. In J. Marques & S. Dhiman (Eds), *Leadership today: Practices for personal and professional development* (pp. 197–216). Springer. doi:10.1007/978-3-319-31036-7_11.
2. Persson, B. N. & Kajonius, P. J. (2016). Empathy and universal values explicated by the empathy–altruism hypothesis. *Journal of Social Psychology*, 156(6), 610–619.
3. Friedkin, N. E. (2004). Social cohesion. *Annual Review of Sociology*, 30, 409–425.
4. Salas, E., Grossman, R., Hughes, A. M. & Coultas, C. W. (2015). Measuring team cohesion. *Human Factors. The Journal of the Human Factors and Ergonomics Society*, 57(3), 365–374.
5. Baker, D. F. (2017). Teaching empathy and ethical decision making in business schools. *Journal of Management Education*, 41(4), 575–598.
6. Zaki, J. (2014). Empathy: A motivated account. *Psychological Bulletin*, 140(6), 1608–1647. doi:10.1037/a0037679
7. Hepper, E. G., Hart, C. M. & Sedikides, C. (2014). Moving Narcissus: Can narcissists be empathic. *Personality and Social Psychology Bulletin*, 40(9), 1079–1091.
8. Atkins, P. W. B. (2013). Empathy, self-other differentiation, and mindfulness training. In K. Pavlovich & K. Krahnke (Eds), *Organizing through empathy* (pp. 61–82). Routledge.
9. Tipsord, J. M. (2009). The effects of mindfulness training and individual differences in mindfulness on social perception and empathy. PhD dissertation, University of Oregon.
10. Thomas, J. T. & Otis, M. D. (2010). Intrapsychic correlates of professional quality of life: Mindfulness, empathy, and emotional separation. *Journal of the Society for Social Work and Research*, 1(2), 83–98 (2010).
11. Decety, J. & Lamm, C. (2007). The role of the right temporoparietal junction in social interaction: How low-level computational processes contribute to meta-cognition. *Neuroscientist*, 13(6), 580–593.

12. Bal, P. M. & Veltkamp, M. (2013). How does fiction reading influence empathy? An experimental investigation on the role of emotional transportation. *PLoS One, 8*(1), e55341.

13. Kinney-Petrucha, M. (2017). "The play's the thing": Theater as an ideal empathy playground. www.researchgate.net/publication/317318081_The_Play's_the_ Thing_Theater_as_an_Ideal_Empathy_Playground

14. Vezzali, L., Stathi, S., Giovannini, D., Capozza, D. & Trifiletti, E. (2015). The greatest magic of Harry Potter: Reducing prejudice. *Journal of Applied Social Psychology, 45*(2), 105–121.

15. Hammond, C. (2019). *The art of rest: How to find respite in the modern age.* Canongate Books.

16. Korbey, H. (2016). How performing in theater can help build empathy in students. | KQED News. www.kqed.org/mindshift/45909/how-performing-in-theater-can-build-empathy-in-students

17. Cuff, B. M. P., Brown, S. J., Taylor, L. & Howat, D. J. (2016). Empathy: A review of the concept. *Emotion Review, 8*(2), 144–153.

18. Kock, N., Mayfield, M., Mayfield, J., Sexton, S. & De La Garza, L. M. E. (2019). Empathetic leadership: How leader emotional support and understanding influences follower performance. *Journal of Leadership and Organizational Studies, 26*(2), 217–236.

19. Heyes, C. (2018). Empathy is not in our genes. *Neuroscience and Biobehavioral Reviews, 95*, 499–507. doi:10.1016/j.neubiorev.2018.11.001

20. De Waal, F. (2009). *The age of empathy: Nature's lessons for a kinder society.* Souvenir Press.

21. Erikson, E. H. (1995). *Childhood and society.* Vintage.

22. Boyatzis, R. E., Passarelli, A. M., Koenig, K., Lowe, M., Mathew, B., Stoller, J. K. & Phillips, M. (2012). Examination of the neural substrates activated in memories of experiences with resonant and dissonant leaders. *Leadership Quarterly, 23*(2), 259–272.

23. Costa, G. & Glinia, E. (2013). Empathy and sport tourism services: A literature review. *Journal of Sport and Tourism, 8*(4), 284–292.

24. van Berkhout, E. T. & Malouff, J. M. (2016). The efficacy of empathy training: A meta-analysis of randomized controlled trials. *Journal of Counseling Psychology, 63*(1), 32–41.

25. Gordon, M. (2012). *Roots of empathy: Changing the world, child by child.* Thomas Allen Publishers.

26. Alexander, J. (2016). America's insensitive children? *The Atlantic.* www. theatlantic.com/education/archive/2016/08/the-us-empathy-gap/494975

27. Cunico, L., Sartori, R., Marognolli, O. & Meneghini, A. M. (2012). Developing empathy in nursing students: A cohort longitudinal study. *Journal of Clinical Nursing, 21*(13/14), 2016–2025.

28. Han, J. L. & Pappas, T. N. (2018). A review of empathy, its importance, and its teaching in surgical training. *Journal of Surgical Education, 75*(1), 88–94.
29. Riess, H., Kelley, J. M., Bailey, R. W., Dunn, E. J. & Phillips, M. (2012). Empathy training for resident physicians: A randomized controlled trial of a neuroscience-informed curriculum. *Journal of General Internal Medicine, 27*(10), 1280–1286.
30. Stepien, K. A. & Baernstein, A. (2006). Educating for empathy: A review. *Journal of General Internal Medicine, 21*(5), 524–530.
31. The Center for Empathy in International Affairs. (2018). World's first empathy training for diplomats. www.centerforempathy.org/worlds-first-empathy-training-for-diplomats
32. Goleman, D., McKee, A. & Achor, S. (2017). *Everyday emotional intelligence: Big ideas and practical advice on how to be human at work.* Harvard Business Review Press.
33. Trout, J. D. (2010). *Why empathy matters: The science and psychology of better judgment.* Penguin Books.
34. Isaacs, W. (1999). *Dialogue and the art of thinking together: A pioneering approach to communicating in business and in life.* Currency/Doubleday.
35. Mazutis, D. & Slawinski, N. (2008). Leading organizational learning through authentic dialogue. *Management Learning, 39*(4), 437–456.
36. Jentz, B. (2007). *Talk sense: Communicating to lead and learn.* Research for Better Teaching.
37. Stanger, N., Kavussanu, M. & Ring, C. P(2012). Put yourself in their boots: Effects of empathy on emotion and aggression. *Journal of Sport and Exercise Psychology, 34*(2), 208–222.
38. Herrera, F., Bailenson, J., Weisz, E., Ogle, E. & Zaki, J. (2018). Building long-term empathy: A large-scale comparison of traditional and virtual reality perspective-taking. *PLoS One, 13*, e0204494.
39. Pavlovich, K. & Krahnke, K. (2012). Empathy, connectedness and organisation. *Journal of Business Ethics, 105*(1), 131–137.
40. Haans, A. & IJsselsteijn, W. (2006). Mediated social touch: A review of current research and future directions. *Virtual Reality, 9*, 149–159.
41. Morrison, I., Löken, L. S. & Olausson, H. (2010). The skin as a social organ. *Experimental Brain Research, 204*(3), 305–314.
42. De Dreu, C. K. W. (2012). Oxytocin modulates cooperation within and competition between groups: An integrative review and research agenda. *Hormones and* Behavior, *61*(3), 419–428.
43. Peled-Avron, L., Levy-Gigi, E., Richter-Levin, G., Korem, N. & Shamay-Tsoory, S. (2016). The role of empathy in the neural responses to observed human social touch. *Cognitive, Affective and Behavioral Neuroscience, 16*(5), 802–813.

44. Goldstein, P., Shamay-Tsoory, S., Yellinek, S. & Weissman-Fogel, I. (2016). Empathy predicts an experimental pain reduction during touch. *Journal of Pain*, *17*(10), 1049–1057.

45. Chatel-Goldman, J., Congedo, M., Jutten, C. & Schwartz, J.-L. (2014). Touch increases autonomic coupling between romantic partners. *Frontiers in Behavioral Neuroscience*, *8*, 95.

46. Christensen, J. F., Gaigg, S. B. & Calvo-Merino, B. (2018). I can feel my heartbeat: Dancers have increased interoceptive accuracy. *Psychophysiology*, *55*(4), e13008.

47. Copeland, R. (2022). Celtic Lisbon Lions voted greatest team EVER as Barcelona and Manchester United don't come close. *The Daily Record*. www.dailyrecord.co.uk/sport/football/celtic-lisbon-lions-voted-greatest-27115508

48. Galipeau, J. & Trudel, P. (2006). Athlete learning in a community of practice: Is there a role for the coach? In R. L. Jones (Ed.), *The sports coach as educator: Re-conceptualising sports coaching* (pp. 95–112). Routledge.

Conclusion

Empathic leaders understand themselves and those they lead. So much so that they can distinguish whose emotions they may be experiencing and predict each team member's behaviour, responses, potential, and suitability for tasks. By employing an empathic approach, leaders can create the right environment for work. Through empathic communication and empathic relationships, emotions can be managed and needs met. In such an environment, team members are empowered, and everyone has a voice. The experience of work is valued, with the aim of job satisfaction and high levels of wellbeing. Team members feel a sense of belonging when they realise they are known and have been accepted by the group. This brings a sense of care and safety to the environment, which enables team members to fulfil their potential and have the confidence to contribute ideas, enhancing creativity. In a working environment like this, retention is unlikely to be a problem and recruitment is facilitated.

This way of leading suits human beings. It is reminiscent of the way of leading that was perfected over a couple of million years, only to be disrupted by technological advances. Human beings once lived in modest, egalitarian hunter-gatherer societies. This way of life lasted for 90 per cent of human history. These societies enjoyed oral cultures within limited geographical areas. For the leaders of these groups, knowing and understanding the individual strengths, weaknesses, talents, and potential of each group member will have been vital for a society to thrive. A large part of a leader's time will have been taken up interacting with each of the group members and continually updating knowledge and understanding.[1]

DOI: 10.4324/9781003324676-9

The development of agriculture, hydraulics, and irrigation allowed societies to grow, covering greater geographic areas with larger populations that needed to be controlled. The work became labour-intensive and required a level of subservience. The knowledge and understanding of the intricacies of each member of the society suddenly had no relevance to leaders who became focused on profits, rather than the survival and prosperity of the group. The Industrial Revolution furthered this trend with societies becoming larger still and social ties more difficult to maintain. Relationships within the group as well as with leaders became more distant. Workers were less empowered and became devalued. They were unlikely to feel that they mattered. Leaders became strangers. This was a process of dehumanisation. Human beings had gone from being valued members of closely knit societies to becoming cogs in the ugly machines of grim factories. Without relationship-focused leader behaviours (like empathy), work may have been appreciated, but workers were not. These are not the circumstances within which people were likely to fulfil their unique potential, provide creativity or innovation, maintain wellbeing, or feel committed to the leaders and organisations they worked for. To the industrialists of the day, this did not matter.

Until the end of the twentieth century, there were still plenty of leaders across industries, including elite sport, who thought that being an autocratic leader, like these industrialists, was the most effective way of motivating teams of people. There are probably leaders who still cling to this style, but they have become an endangered species. After a couple of centuries of autocratic leadership, a realisation grew that a more human way of leading allows workers to be more engaged and to offer far more to their teams and organisations. The potentials of individuals have become of interest again to leaders. A realisation that it is important to understand people and their thoughts and feelings. The change has gathered pace, and now empathy has become the most sought-after leadership skill.

Leadership has become more about shared visions and less about control.[2] Workers are being described as partners or collaborators.[3] And working climates are becoming safer.

In elite sport, the tide has certainly turned. Leaders of teams now focus on the same things that leaders of groups of hunter-gatherers focused on, knowing and understanding the individual strengths, weaknesses, talents, and potential that exists across a group. A leader has to constantly engage with group members, not only to maintain knowledge and understanding but also to display empathy.[1]

Studies across industries have shown that leaders who display empathy are more effective leaders than those who do not. However, the emotionally challenging environment of elite sport is a unique context for an empathic leadership style.

Head coaches in elite sport have incorporated greater displays of empathy in their leadership, focusing on managing emotions in order to maintain safe climates, which can impact on team performance. For example, head coaches understand the significance of their touchline behaviour and that it may influence the emotions of competing athletes. They also described using empathic communication to create emotional bonds and close relationships with those they lead. In these relationships, head coaches use every opportunity to keep their information up to date through informal conversations, and by focusing on listening to those they lead. The levels of mutual knowledge and understanding obtained help to avoid the kind of misunderstandings that can ruin careers. Communication is tailored to the extent of leaders consulting team members about preferred timing and methods, such as video call, text, telephone or face to face, with the latter always being preferred by leaders. Face-to-face communication provides another opportunity to learn more about an individual. Facial expressions, body language, and tone of voice can all be missed out on in other modes of communication.

In the closer relationships that leaders enjoy in elite sport, trust is elevated, and close connections have positive influences on wellbeing. However, the boundaries between a head coach and athletes can become blurred, and an ideal distance has to be maintained. This helps to fend off bias or accusations of favouritism from other group members. Getting too close to individual athletes can make decision making concerning things such as selection a difficult task. The situation can be further complicated by gender differences between the head coach and athletes.

In close relationships, there is likely to be more physical contact. We see head coaches physically interacting with their athletes all the time on our television screens, in ways that were less familiar a decade or two ago. This may be unique to sport. Leaders in other industries maybe less inclined to be in regular physical contact with team members. But in elite sport, there is no greater example of a close relationship than the post-match hug. Head coaches noted that the athlete's perspective always needs to be considered in such instances and that the leader's behaviour needs to be authentic.

In order to make the right judgements about hugging athletes, head coaches need to maintain high levels of empathic accuracy. This allows them to empathise in order to understand how such behaviour will be received. Head coaches also use empathic accuracy to help predict how an athlete will perform in a certain situation, how they will react to particular events, and what their potential is going forward.

A head coach working in elite sport today has a multitude of relationships to manage. There are larger squad sizes and more assistants, media, managers, fans groups, and officials than at any time in the history of sport. They also have relationships with rival coaches to maintain. The head coaches I have spoken to explained that by knowing a rival head coach, it is easier to empathise with them accurately. This brings knowledge and understanding of the opposition. Their intentions, motivations, and strategies will be easier to grasp, allowing the empathic leader to counteract and gain an edge.

With an athlete-centred focus, a head coach places emphasis on athlete wellbeing. Athlete wellbeing is sought by head coaches of elite teams in sport due to its link with performance, and empathy is recognised to be supportive of health. When team members feel more cared for, leaders become more popular, which allows them greater levels of power and influence. Perceived empathy makes a leader more appreciated and heightens commitment towards them and their causes.

Empathic leaders understand that empathy within a team can be just as powerful, and they work on developing empathy through on-field and off-field activities. Developing empathy within teams helps to build team cohesion. This is often achieved by asking athletes to share biographical stories with their teammates. Swapping roles during training allows athletes to understand the challenges faced by their teammates and gain knowledge of the perspectives of those they pass to so that their delivery can be more appropriate. And in order to gain a better understanding of the opposition, athletes can watch their past performances on video and be tasked with competing with athletes of a similar style in training.

I have often asked the head coaches I have met what their main aims are in leadership. Their responses have included: developing a safe climate; understanding individual athletes; enhancing commitment and trust; increasing team cohesion; encouraging wellbeing; satisfying expectations; enhancing creativity; predicting reactions, performances, and potential; and improving performance. As you will now understand, all of these can be successfully pursued through a more empathic approach.

Leaders are often tasked with recognising leadership qualities in others.[4] If the values of an empathic leader run true, empathy is likely to be valued in those considered for leadership roles. In team sport, the head coach is often tasked with recruiting captains and creating leadership groups.[5] By choosing an empathic captain, a leader can encourage empathy to spread through the group. The context of sport is unique in that a head coach cannot actively lead the team during competition on the field of play. When choosing a leader within the team, all the head coaches I have spoken to have told me that they take empathic qualities into consideration. Head coaches understand that an empathic leadership style helps to maintain a safe climate in elite sport, off the pitch as much as on it.

There are claims across industries including elite sport that empathy has become expected of leaders. One of the dangers of not providing the empathy that is expected is the loss of talent. The kind of leadership more familiar in past eras, which lacked empathy, is unlikely to be tolerated by contemporary athletes, and if options are available for them to move on, they will. It is also worth remembering that in the context of elite sport, the reputations of leaders can attract or repel the best talent.

To maintain an empathic leadership style, the head coach needs to commit to developing empathy in themselves and expressing it in all situations in order to be viewed as authentic. Empathic leadership should not be viewed as a style that can be immediately adopted from a textbook. Empathic skills need to be worked on and this takes time. This will involve mentalising, practising listening, refining communication skills, and engaging in other practices known to develop empathy, such as reading fiction or engaging with other narrative art.

Empathic leaders should be considered assets to sport organisations because they are able to maintain close relationships, safe climates, commitment, job satisfaction, wellbeing, team cohesion, and attract talent. Forget any misconceptions you may have of empathy being a so-called soft skill or that it makes a leader weak. Empathic leaders become strong leaders, through respect, appreciation, and behaviours such as listening, which enhances their prestige. Empathy inspires team members to go above and beyond their obligations. Ultimately, this means that the empathic leader yields more power.

Empathy development training is becoming a feature of all industries that involve people and relationships at work. Sport should not be left behind. Coach programmes should include empathy development, and sport organisations should be looking to develop empathy in young coaches and, indeed, athletes. Empathy should become a major focus of training programmes because the successful leadership of teams in elite sport is dependent on relationships, understanding, and motivating people. Having read to the end of this book, you should now understand what it takes to become an empathic leader. It is a style of leadership that suits us as human beings and allows potentials to be fulfilled. I hope that what you have read will prove helpful and wish you well in all of your endeavors.

Notes

1. Rifkin, J. (2010). The empathic civilization – An address before the British Royal Society for the Arts– Part I: Rethinking human nature and the history of the human journey on the cusp of the biosphere era. www.youtube.com/watch?v=1-7BjeHepbA
2. Northouse, P. G. (2015). *Leadership: Theory and practice.* Sage Publications.
3. Reicher, S., Haslam, S. A. & Hopkins, N. (2005). Social identity and the dynamics of leadership: Leaders and followers as collaborative agents in the transformation of social reality. *Leadership Quarterly, 16*(4), 547–568.
4. Dinh, J. E., Lord, R. G., Gardner, W. L., Meuser, J. D., Liden, R. C. & Hu, J. (2014). Leadership theory and research in the new millennium: Current theoretical trends and changing perspectives. *Leadership Quarterly, 25*(1), 36–62.
5. Light Shields, D. L., Gardner, D. E., Light Bredemeier, B. J. & Bostro, A. (1997). The relationship between leadership behaviors and group cohesion in team sports. *Journal of Psychology: Interdisciplinary and Applied, 131*(2), 196–210.

Bonus Material

So much of what I have learned from head coaches in elite sport did not make it into the main text of this book. I thought it would be useful to provide some more examples of their wisdom and experience to reflect on. The following quotes should resonate far more having read this book.

"I first came back to the club for an opportunity to be second-team coach. I said, 'I'll do it, but I want to do it my way.' I said, 'Look, I've played for a lot of coaches, I think the second-team environment can be quite poisonous . . .' The thing that was there the whole time for me was authenticity and having an empathic side and understanding actually what I want to do is to develop people. The cricket is the second bit. If we can evolve the character of the individual, the cricket will take care of itself."

Men's cricket head coach

"I worked as an assistant to a head coach before becoming a head coach myself. And he set a fine example, I must say. I don't know if he'd always been the same or if he developed his style, but I soon realised that he had totally mastered man-management. I guess now you'd call it empathy. He understood people. Knew what made them tick. I saw how much love the players had for him, and that's not over the top. It was love. They didn't just love him as a head coach; they loved him as a human being. To those players, he was a father figure; he gave what all good fathers give – care and understanding. I saw grown men cry when he left. It must have been like losing a father. His man-management was the best I've seen in any head coach. He treated the players as human beings, whether they won or lost. Even his training sessions showed how much he got people. I think these kinds of people are rare, but they have existed in the past. Although the emphasis on that kind of approach is more evident now. It's what most coaches aspire to."

Men's football head coach, North America

"Interestingly, there are others in the sport, and I report to a perform-ance director and to people higher up the food chain. Players missing training is a red rag to a bull to them; they see it in very black-and-white terms, you know. You're either in or you're out. And I was under a lot of pressure to make different decisions, and I'm no longer the national coach. I'd stood up for the players on a number of occasions, and some of those decisions have probably, ultimately, cost me my job as the national coach."

Men's international lacrosse head coach

"I have no problem about taking all the time in the world to explain, when I need to, but if we disagree and have very different ideas, then I have to convince them that my idea is better than theirs. There is a chance that they might convince me that their idea is better. That's not so bad. We get to improve something, great. It must be a two-way conversation. It is all about that great power of listening."

Women's international volleyball head coach

"Women will remember what you've said to them three months ago, and some of them will bring notepads with them to meetings, and they jot things down and you're thinking, 'Well, I really need to be careful of what I say.' Your level of conversation and thought process has to be more considered. I've said do this and she'll say, 'Back in November, you said do this . . .' So, on and off the field, you need to really think about how they'll hear you, and they'll ask you questions, and expect answers, and if you contradict yourself, they'll tell you. They'll listen more closely too; they'll follow instructions better too. You need to both appreciate and be aware of this as a coach."

Women's international football head coach

"It's massive, the difference. Women are much more sensitive than men. I can have a stand-up row with somebody – you may have got that about me. With men, they forget that within ten seconds. I can be tougher in some ways with girls, but I'm always more careful about how I say things. It can have an adverse effect on their performance. They can carry it, and for months. If you find yourself in the situation again, they remember the last time and it's worse. So I keep the language positive, and it's really chalk and cheese. I enjoy coaching both, but it's very different."

Men's international handball head coach

"I have understanding due to my own experiences, so I can empathise. I nearly stopped playing when I had to move from boys' football to girls'. The boys were accepting and easy. It was simple. Whereas in the female teams it was, like, horrible; they felt their places were under threat, and they'd go into bitch mode, and I felt isolated as the new person. And when I do presentations, I often speak about that. For a new female to go to a sports club or fitness class and they see established groups, it's the one reason they don't go back. And maybe some men are the same, but I nearly stopped playing for that reason, and I know it's still happening to lots of girls coming through. Because our friend groups and social groups are men. Because you've always played football, you've always hung out with boys until you're 14 or so. Then you lose your core social group. You're not allowed to stay with them any more, and it becomes a really difficult time. I think that's why a lot of girls stop playing."

Women's football head coach

"There's definitely a difference between male and female coaching. I was once brought to task by the female coaches that I worked with. They were, like, you can't talk to people like that!

"There are so many differences. Women like selection notifications via email and then have the conversations when they are ready and that actually makes it easier for me. I told them I'd telephone them for the first game's selection, and they said, 'No! Don't call us.' They told me to email them. I thought, 'I won't object to this, that's saved me five very difficult conversations. They will have a chat to me, but when they are ready, on their terms, and that's fine.' That's very different to men. We have looked at what we do that's right psychologically for the women, compared to the men. That's tracking my evolution into a head coach of women. How you handle off-the-field situations is the same, it's vital."

Women's international rugby union head coach

"We can be real bitches. Women are unkinder to each other than in male-to-female relationships. I think they understand each other better, but sometimes they are so cutting. If there was a group of women sitting over there, straight away they get this vibe, of whether they are really nice, or they are looking you up and down and make you feel the size of a pea, in that one look. Some women just don't like other women. Men have a fight and then go for a pint. With women, they need to watch their backs for the next ten years. It's really interesting how women want to be portrayed as strong and independent, but at the same time the aftermath of that. Recently, I let a player go, and there's dig after dig after dig in the media and online. Whereas a guy will find another team and just go and get on with it. We want to be strong, but then we want to be vulnerable. I'm not saying men aren't vulnerable, but they are very different. I think that's the most important thing for coaches to understand."

Women's football head coach

"I do find female players to be different to male players, though. They are more communicative. Closer isn't probably the right word, but I can't think of another one; it's a different relationship with females. It's more honest, 100 per cent more honest, and sometimes they'll talk themselves down – too much honesty, you know. They communicate differently. We could be in a room of guys watching a game on TV and not say anything to each other, whereas women will chat away. The type of communication is different, so then that gives them a closer personal relationship between the women because of that different dynamic."

International women's football head coach

"Sometimes we'll lose a game, and a player will put on social media 'Great to get 90 mins' or 'Great to get a goal', and that's just individual. Everyone else and the general feeling is quite down, and you are just talking about *you*. Certain clubs will only put things out or tweet if they win. And interviews too, only if they win. I think that lacks integrity and people soon see through it. We have to consider how it looks."

Women's football head coach

"Sometimes I don't predict accurately. Particularly when it comes to emotional reactions. We got into both finals again and we had got better, and we won them both this time. Then you think you'll be happy forever and the joy is going to be . . . and that didn't happen. Four days after, everybody was suffering the same anti-climax, and once we got together as a group, we realised that okay, it wasn't the trophy that gave you the joy and the . . . We kind of committed to each other that our daily experience here has to be the thing."

Men's rugby union head coach

"We looked at how they played recently, but also tried to estimate by saying if we were them and were playing us, what would we do, where would you think we were vulnerable . . . If we agree that we are vulnerable there, well, let's make sure we are not vulnerable there, regardless of what they do. That will be a problem otherwise for us. So, empathising with rival coaches allows us to think about any weaknesses our end. We also get lots of feedback from the players, a lot of whom have played against these players. We recently played against a team that one of our players had done pre-season with, so she had some insight to them. The goalkeeper we played against at the weekend I had at a former club, so I had information on her to share."

Women's football head coach

"What I've found now is that with the more you get to know them, the more you understand if they are a process person: do they work by feel, are they an easy-going person? So, we've done a lot of psychological profiling like Spotlight, which is about discovering the make-up of people. Whether they are bouncy characters, empathic, directive. That's shaped how we communicate with them. Particularly when we are putting a new squad together, this helps from coaching point of view, but it's only a starting point."

Men's international lacrosse head coach

"I don't know if other players felt like this, but you often don't know what you are good at. I think back and it was only a few times. I was always quick, always in the top two or three in the team, but I never realised until someone told me. They said, 'You know how quick you are,' and I said, 'Well, no.' Well, yeah, you can use that to take on players and then I started doing that. So someone helping you understand yourself. Managers who made it clear what your strengths were. And I try to do that now."

Women's international football head coach

"Selecting teams for the Olympics, having conversations with people, telling them after two years' training that they are not coming, that is a very tough conversation to have, but nowhere near as hard as it is to hear. I know how they feel because I've been there, so I'm ready for their reaction."

Women's international rugby union head coach

"Experience obviously helped me understand players more accurately. I had a couple of really tough experiences. One, I was left out of a cup final, playing in a final, every kid's dream; I played in every game up to it and got left out. It was probably the best experience I could have had as a player because it showed me what you have to do to stay in a team and how you have to address your shortfalls."

Women's football head coach

"I think I have a natural tendency to be empathic, but I think anyone can learn it. I think it's something that can come into your coaching. I mean, I've been working with a coach in Norway, and she'd won everything, and I saw her in a situation coaching players where she almost can't understand why they don't train like she does. I think that's something that, in a year or two, she'll understand. And that will help her not be frustrated, massively."

Women's international hockey head coach

"It's a really interesting topic because you look at psychological profiling and look at the red, green, blue, yellow; I think the older generation was more: red, directive, this is how it goes. And then you add to that as you get to know them as people. And the modern era wants that leadership, but also wants someone who's got that feel for people . . . I mean, if I had to be a leader in the French Foreign Legion, that's not me, I couldn't do it. They'd see right through me, it's not me."

Men's international rugby union head coach

"I think empathy plays a huge role in leadership; I believe it does anyway. We brought in two girls from another team and their reaction to how I was . . . was big, because their former coach wasn't very empathic towards them, and they were surprised . . . Their reactions were good, they were much more open. They said they felt much more comfortable. One told me she didn't feel nervous to call me with questions on this and that."

Women's ice hockey head coach

"I believe in working with people as human beings; I see them as human first and not a player. So the relationship side is incredibly important to me. Understanding them emotionally and trying to gauge where they are . . . I don't like to give you an example because it's happening all the time. It's a big part of who I am and how I operate."

Men's cricket head coach

"I always say this: in my first year pro, I won everything possible. All the possible titles in my first year, so I left right away. I thought there's nothing I have to do in that organisation any more; they'd never won before and now they'd won everything. So I built a team from scratch; they had only youth players, but no professional team at all. I started from ground zero and built it into a successful organisation. People think I'm proud of this sort of thing, sure I am, but I find the biggest achievements of my coaching career came at the beginning when I coached kids: one kid who wasn't very talented, but was willing to pay the price, so we as a coaching staff managed to teach him how to work hard, and what hard work means, and we made him so dedicated that he worked harder than anyone. So he had the best tests in the country, but he still wasn't skilled enough to play the game. But he'd learned how to work hard. When he quit, he studied to be a doctor and he had the best grades in the whole university. So I think we, as staff, had a huge part in that success. I could go on with these examples. This is my Stanley Cup; these are the things that are very important to me."

Men's ice hockey head coach

"We are a small sport. That means everyone knows each other – a lot got into the sport because their dad played in men's lacrosse, certainly. That means geographically they seem to be similar types of persons from similar environments, but we can really play on that and when the proverbial hits the fan, and that happens a lot to us as a team. When we were at the World Championships, we were down in a number of games, and by insurmountable amounts, but probably notably in one game we were just blown away, we were down 8–0, which is probably the equivalent of being 4–0 down in football. Being battered, couldn't touch the ball. And other teams have folded and disappeared up their own backsides, but this team, that idea that they're family kept them going."

Men's international lacrosse head coach

"I'm conscious that I want to share my vision. So, for example, when people come to the gate, and the gate men are rude, and they represent the club like that, that reflects on us. It's important they understand what we're trying to do. A fan might come in and say they are a shit team, right now. I want the guy on the gate to say, 'Well, you should see how good they've been in training this week.' It's important to communicate with the wider group; you need everyone on side."

Men's cricket head coach

"We have five owners, but they are not making money out of this; they are dedicated in time and money and want to make the team successful – it's their hobby. They come to the games; they want to have fun and feel part of something that's growing and becoming more successful. Their perspective is very different. So what I have to do is push them and make them understand how things work, while keeping them involved, and so they keep interested and giving their money and time. I'm balancing, and many times it's tough because other teams have more money than we do, but the environment we've created is one that players want to be involved in, and that's what makes us successful."

Men's ice hockey head coach

"I'm a huge fan of one of our players. I suggested we made him captain at 23, reasons being, he's going to be an outstanding leader, he's just starting to establish himself, and actually he epitomises everything we are trying to do. I'm sick of foreign players coming in and captaining. They are good, but too often they don't buy into what you are trying to do; they can't – they don't understand the fabric of the organisation."

Men's cricket head coach

"We've got a lot of players that have come from other clubs. So it's important that they know this particular team and what it stands for. Our whole start to the season was about finding out where we were at. Some people had never lived in this city before. Our overseas players had never lived in this country before. We've got two British passport holders that have lived in two different countries, so you know, trying to get them to understand what this place is about was our first focus, and what is important. So it was about giving people understanding about the psyche behind our team."

Women's netball head coach

"When I see my players play for national sides, it's about how they represent themselves when they are away. That's the most rewarding thing. Because the feedback we get is 'Oh, what an unbelievable character, what a great bloke,' and the cricket side comes second. So that makes me feel I've done a good job."

Men's cricket head coach

"I'm not a big football fan, but since I moved to Europe, I follow Liverpool. I have much respect for how die-hard the fans are in England for their clubs. Jürgen Klopp's leadership style, he is a very modern coach – you can see the players trust him, even the ones who don't play so much. That is so important, especially at that level where they are paid millions and millions of pounds, that if you are not playing, you still have that trust of your leader . . . When they won the Champions League, the guys who looked the happiest weren't even selected for the game, but Klopp made them feel so loved and part of the team. His leadership style is so impressive. I have lived in Sweden for a few years, but we only have two non-Swedes in the team, and they understand the culture, but for Klopp, the cultural differences are huge, massive, different languages, and for them to all be on the same page is massive . . . Liverpool's success is obviously down to them being a great team, but also Klopp should get so much credit for the way he has used empathy and trust and the belief they have in him . . . When they talk to him, I'd bet he talks to them a lot about their children, their wives, their lives, you know. He wants to understand them and their perspective. That's empathy."

Women's ice hockey head coach

Index

head coaches 7–8; ability to adapt
rapidly 29; appropriate language
use 37–38; Chinese experience
59; dealing with disagreements
133; hubristic attitude 34; need for
empathy 11, 12; need for mentors
26–27; relations with hierarchy
61–62; shortness of tenure 28; use of
team games 116–117
hugging 55–57; and empathic accuracy
125; gender differences 58–59;
oxytocin release 114
human beings: early 123–124

impression cues: examples 98; sources
97; use 97–98
Industrial Revolution 124
inner world: exploration of 19–20;
see also daydreaming

job satisfaction 51, 70, 84, 89, 111, 123;
see also wellbeing
judgement suspension: and self-
empathy 22
Jung, Carl: on water as symbol of
unconscious mind 19

Lawrence, T.E.: on daydreaming 21
leaders: expectations of millennials 6;
need for empathy 11, 124–125, 127
leadership: athlete-centred approach
82–84; autocratic 5, 124; groups 54;
in politics 10; qualities, recognition of
126; and shared vision 124; in sport
7; style, example 158; worker-centred
81; *see also* empathic leadership
learning disability: dealing with 92
life experiences: and empathy 110–111
listening skills 11, 133; and
communication 35; culturally
cognizant 36; fidelity 37; mutual
active 38; and wellbeing influencing
35–36
losing: dealing with 152

Mandela, Nelson: *Conversations with
Myself* 24; empathic leadership
24–25; stoicism 24
Maslow's Hierarchy of Needs 87

meditation: beginning 23; and
wellbeing 22
mental illness: confidentiality 91–92;
cortisol levels 90; elite athletes 89
mentalising *see* perspective taking
mentors: head coaches need for
26–27
millennials: expectations of leaders 6
mistakes: admitting 70
misunderstandings: avoidance of 36

negotiations: cognitive empathy in 10

oxytocin release: hugging 114

penalty kicks: pressure situations
102–103
perceived empathy 28, 85–89; and
commitment 85
performance: and innovation 70; and
wellbeing 89, 126
personal presentations: empathy
training 113–114
perspective taking: cognitive empathy
10, 106; empathy training 112
physical contact: empathic leadership
55–57, 125
pity 9
positive empathy 8
potential recognition 99–101
power: and empathy 34
preconscious mind 19; accessing 22
problem recognition: empathic leaders
101
psychological profiling 50, 143, 148
psychological safety 67–68, 70
psychology: use of 88
psychopathy 10

reflection time: and emotions 74
relationships: breakdowns 92–93;
multiple 59–63, 126
remembering: gender differences 134
resilience: and empathy 116
rivals: body language of 106, 107;
emotional climate of 106–107;
understanding 105–107, 126, 142
Rogers, Carl 67
role playing: empathy training 112, 126

Printed in the United States
by Baker & Taylor Publisher Services